In Good Time

FINE FOOD IN UNDER AN HOUR

DESIGN
Megantic Design

TITLE LETTERING
Barry Lavender

COVER PHOTOGRAPH
Canada à la Carte magazine
Simon Cheung, Photographer

ARTWORK
Martha Bull

COPY EDITOR
Peggy McKee

FOOD EDITOR
Joan Mackie

TYPESETTING
Jay Tee Graphics Ltd.

COLOUR SEPARATION
Formart Graphics

CAMERA
John Ormsby

GRAPHICS SUPPLIES
Allworth Ltd.

PRINTING
Webcom

This cookbook is dedicated to the Barbra Schlifer Commemorative Clinic—to the Board of Directors, its staff and most especially the women who use its services.

The Clinic opened its doors in September 1985, providing a unique blend of legal and counselling services for women who experience any kind of violence. It was established in memory of Barbra Schlifer, who was sexually assaulted and murdered on April 11, 1980, the day of her call to the Bar of Ontario.

Free legal and counselling services are offered to battered women, incest survivors, sexual assault victims and women who have been harrassed at work. The Clinic's programs have been acknowledged by scores of agencies which refer women who have experienced violence.

The Cookbook Committee is pleased to provide these recipes and this book to benefit the Barbra Schlifer Commemorative Clinic. The proceeds will support the programs of the Clinic.

CONTENTS

The Cookbook Committee

CO-ORDINATORS

Anita Fineberg
Joan Garson
Carol MacPherson

COMMITTEE MEMBERS

Erika Abner
Susan Baskin
June Borgmann
Debra Campbell
Kristine Connidis
Judy Coviensky
Carol Garson
Marilyn Garson
Sandra Taube Godard
Julie Hannaford

Joan Johannson
Barbara MacPherson
Leslie McIntyre
Evelyn McKee
Glenna Munro
Edie Neuberger
Susan Reid
Elaine Rouch
Jennifer Sunley

Thanks to...

Many people assisted us in producing *In Good Time*. We would like especially to thank the following:

Julia Aitken
Andres Wine
Eleanor Ball
David Baskin
Joan Bentley
Silvia Berno
Mr. and Mrs. David Campbell
Vicky Campbell
Lucille Chaplan
Harbord Bakery
Annette D'Arcy
Gay Harper
Lynn Johnston
Judy Leach
Sid Markowski
Ed Nodwell
Loretta Pompilio
Irene Szylinger
Theatre Passe Muraille
Gloria Varley
Ron Zerafa

Patrons

Erika Abner

Bob Adler and Cheryl Shour-Adler

M. Elizabeth Atcheson

Donna J. Baptist & Associates,
Personnel Consultants

Janis Barlow

David Baskin

Marjorie Baskin

Susan Baskin

Varda Berenstein

Bowring Gift Shops

Martha Bull

Barry Campbell

Mr. and Mrs. David Campbell

Debra Grobstein Campbell

Community Involvement Team
Rexdale D.C., Great Northern
Apparel Inc.

Community Occupational Therapy
Associates

Kristine Connidis

Contacts

Carol Cruikshank

George and Lynne Czutrin

Eiderdown Shop

Joan Eiley

Sheila and Jeff Engel

Anita Fineberg

Mr. and Mrs. Elliot Fineberg

Sybil Fineberg

Joan H. Finlayson

Carol Garson and
Sidney Markowski

Joan Garson

Lily Garson

The Garson Family

Sandra Taube and Fred Godard

Bryna Goldberg and
Howard Harris

Harry Grobstein

Ed Gulbinas

Barbara Hall, Alderman,
City of Toronto

Julie Hannaford

Leslie A. Hill

HMC Computer Corporation

Hogan & Greenfield Design
Build Ltd.

Anna Jagielo

Jennifer's Kitchen Ltd.

Joan and Sven Johannson

Bruce Keleher, Leslie Mendelson
and Alex Keleher

Kellogg Salada Canada Inc.

Dr. Michael and Barbara Lefcoe

Lipton's

Ellen MacDonald

Michael A. MacDonald

Barbara MacPherson

Carol MacPherson

Dorothy MacPherson

James MacPherson

Marguerite Markowski

Leslie McIntyre

David A. McKee

Evelyn McKee

Cliodhna McMullin

Donna Montador

Nancy M. Mossip

Glenn and Sonya Munro

S. John Page

Jim and Jean Reid and Family

Susan Reid
Martin Richards
Leslie Ritz-Campbell
Elaine Rouch
Carole J. Salomon
Dr. Eva Saxell-Johnson
Jay Shepherd
Ada Schermann
Goldie Schermann
Philip Spencer
R.B. Stapells
Jennifer Sunley
The Woman's Show Ltd.
Third Thursday Network
Marina Ushycky
Toby Vigod
Nancy Wardle
Trudy M. White
Lilly Wong
Debora, Michael and
    Sara Zatzman
Zonta Club of Mississauga

Introduction

In Good Time is a cookbook for busy people. It has been compiled for cooks who have little time but lots of desire to present tasty, attractive and unusual food to family and friends.

We on the Cookbook Committee believe it is possible to prepare and serve fine food in under an hour without 'welding', that is, opening two cans and combining the contents in a pot. We are not denying the utility of many canned products; there are recipes in the book which include them. However, our approach is that fresh and freshly prepared food is preferable whenever possible.

You may be surprised at the wealth of recipes in each category. We were excited by the number of delicious soups and spectacular desserts which fitted into our time frame. Our own bias in favour of light and healthy food also influenced the selection of recipes.

We intend the book to be useful for any time you need a recipe, for all courses of the meal and for most occasions when home cooked food is included. Each recipe category includes food for family and for entertaining. Many of the recipes will work equally well as one element of a meal or as its main course.

Our recipes do not require the use of food processors or microwave ovens. Obviously, there are stages in some recipes in which these appliances can be used to reduce preparation or cooking time. We have arbitrarily included recipes requiring standing and freezing time in excess of the one-hour limit; your time and attention are not required during this period.

We have also collected the special tips each of us on the committee use to reduce preparation and cooking time. You'll find these in the section entitled 'Tips for Living'.

A lot of hard work has gone into publishing the book—despite which, we have enjoyed ourselves immensely. We thank our friends, families and colleagues, for contributing recipes and for being guinea pigs in an extensive recipe testing process. All testers can now go back to eating without pondering whether their food is 'visually appealing' or 'extraordinarily good'!

We could not have printed the book without the generosity of our patrons and other supporters. We also thank everyone who donated time, expertise and services to the successful completion of this project; we have tried to list everyone who helped us in the preceding pages. We apologize to anyone whose name was accidently omitted; you know nevertheless how much your assistance was appreciated.

If you have as good a time in using the book as we did in compiling it, we have succeeded in our intent. We hope the recipes will enable you to leave the kitchen in good time for sharing our food with family and friends.

FIRSTS

Addictive Dip

This dip is as delicious as its name suggests. It is also incredibly simple to prepare. The dip will taste better if prepared the day before so that the flavours become well blended.

PREPARATION TIME: 15 minutes
YIELD: 2 cups (500 mL)

2 cloves	garlic, minced	2 cloves
2 Tbsp	chopped fresh parsley	25 mL
2 Tbsp	minced onion	25 mL
1 cup	sour cream	250 mL
1/4 cup	mayonnaise	50 mL
2	eggs, hard-boiled	2
	paprika	

Combine the garlic, parsley, onion, sour cream and mayonnaise. Separate the eggs. Grate the whites and add to the mixture. Transfer to a serving bowl. Crumble the yolks and sprinkle on top. Dust with paprika.

Serve at room temperature with raw vegetables or crackers.

Variation: Dijon mustard may be added for a perkier and more addictive dip.

Artichoke Dip

Piping hot and inviting, this unusual dip is hard to resist when presented, as suggested, in a round loaf of black bread.

PREPARATION TIME: 10 minutes
COOKING TIME: 50 minutes
YIELD: 8-10 servings

1	round loaf of black bread	1
1 can (14-oz)	artichoke hearts, drained	1 can (398 mL)
1 cup	grated Parmesan cheese	250 mL
1/4 cup	mayonnaise	50 mL
3/4 cup	plain yogurt	175 mL
1/4 tsp	lemon juice	1 mL
dash	black pepper	dash

Preheat the oven to 375°F (190°C).

Slice the top off the loaf of bread. Scoop out the interior and cut into 1-inch (2.5 cm) chunks. Reserve the chunks.

Combine the remaining ingredients in a blender or food processor. Spoon the mixture into the hollow loaf and replace the top. Wrap the loaf in foil and bake for 50 minutes.

Serve with the reserved bread chunks, for dipping. (The top can also be cut up and dipped into the mixture.)

Variation: Individual dips can be made using black or rye rolls and reducing baking time to about 30 minutes.

Tarragon Dip

Because this flavourful dip is so easy to prepare, it is ideal to serve to those friends who just happen to drop by.

PREPARATION TIME: 10 minutes
YIELD: 1 cup (250 mL)

3/4 cup	mayonnaise	175 mL
2 Tbsp	grated Parmesan cheese	25 mL
1 tsp	dry mustard	5 mL
1 1/2 Tbsp	tarragon vinegar	20 mL
	fresh tarragon or parsley as garnish	

Combine ingredients. Garnish with fresh sprigs of tarragon or parsley. Chill.

Serve with raw vegetables such as cauliflower, green and red peppers, radishes, cucumbers, zucchini and green onions.

Sinful Shrimp Dip

Such a rich and tangy dip is sure to be a real crowd pleaser.

PREPARATION TIME: 15 minutes
YIELD: 2 cups (500 mL)

2 Tbsp	finely chopped onion	25 mL
8 oz	cream cheese, room temperature	250 g
1/3 cup	ketchup or chili sauce	75 mL
2 Tbsp	lemon juice	25 mL
2 Tbsp	horseradish	25 mL
1 tsp	Worcestershire sauce	5 mL
3-4 drops	Tabasco sauce	3-4 drops
2 cans (4-oz)	cocktail-size shrimp	2 cans (125 g)

Combine all the ingredients except for shrimp.

Rinse the shrimp under cold running water and drain well. Fold the shrimp into the dip mixture.

Serve cold with crackers or crisp celery and zucchini sticks.

Crab Dip

Coconut and crab combine to create a distinct 'island' flavour.

PREPARATION TIME: **10 minutes**
YIELD: **2 1/2 cups (625 mL)**

1 can	crab meat, drained	1 can
(4-oz)		(125 g)
1/2-3/4 cup	coconut	125-175 mL
1/2 pt	sour cream	250 mL
1/2 cup	mayonnaise	125 mL
4	scallions, finely chopped	4
2 tsp	curry powder	10 mL
1 drop	Tabasco sauce	1 drop
1/4 tsp	lime juice (optional)	1 mL
	parsley as garnish	

Combine all the ingredients and chill well prior to serving.

Garnish with parsley and serve with crackers.

This dip will keep well in the refrigerator for 1 week.

Crab Pâté

Impress your guests with this easy-to-prepare gourmet appetizer.

PREPARATION TIME: 10 minutes
YIELD: 2 1/2 cups (625 mL)

1 pkg (8-oz)	cream cheese	1 pkg (250 g)
2 Tbsp	chili sauce	25 mL
1 Tbsp	Tabasco sauce	15 mL
2 tsp	lemon juice	10 mL
2 cans	crabmeat, drained	2 cans
(7-oz)		(198 g)
2 Tbsp	minced scallions	25 mL
2 Tbsp	minced fresh parsley	25 mL

Beat the cream cheese, chili sauce, Tabasco and lemon juice until the mixture is smooth. Combine with the crab, scallions and parsley.

Serve with crackers or thin slices of rye bread. The pâté can be eaten immediately, but the flavour improves if it is prepared an hour prior to serving.

Incredibly Easy Pâté

Don't let the eccentricity of the ingredients stop you from trying this recipe. You will be pleasantly surprised by the results.

PREPARATION TIME: 15 minutes
REFRIGERATION TIME: 2 hours
YIELD: 1 1/2 cups (375 mL)

8 oz	liverwurst, room temperature	250 g
2 Tbsp	finely chopped onion	25 mL
2 Tbsp	mayonnaise	25 mL
1 tsp	sherry	5 mL
	pepper to taste	
8 oz	cream cheese	250 g
2 Tbsp	18% cream	25 mL
	chives, chopped	

Beat liverwurst until smooth. Add the onion, mayonnaise, sherry and pepper and mix until the flavours are blended. Add more mayonnaise if mixture is too stiff.

Line a small bowl with clear plastic wrap. Pack the liverwurst into the bowl and cover with excess wrap.

Chill for 2 hours.

Whip the cream cheese and cream until spreadable. Turn the liverwurst upside down onto a serving plate and remove the wrap. Frost the pâté with the cream cheese. Sprinkle the top with chives.

Deluxe Pâté

Since this recipe freezes well, double the quantity and have it on hand for unexpected guests.

PREPARATION TIME: 20 minutes
MARINATING TIME: 1 1/2 hours
COOKING TIME: 10 minutes
REFRIGERATION TIME: 4 hours
YIELD: 2 cups (500 mL)

8 oz	chicken livers	250 g
1 cup	Madeira	250 mL
2 Tbsp	butter	25 mL
6 slices	bacon, chopped	6 slices
2	green onions, chopped	2
1/2 tsp	thyme	2 mL
1/4 cup	35% cream	50 mL
2 Tbsp	sherry	25 mL
1 tsp	brandy	5 mL
1/2 tsp	salt	2 mL
4 turns	fresh black pepper	4 turns

Marinate the chicken livers in the Madeira for 1 1/2 hours. Drain and pat dry, reserving 2 tablespoons (25 mL) of Madeira.

Sauté the livers in butter until light on the outside and pink on the inside—about 3 to 4 minutes.

In a separate frying pan, fry the bacon until almost cooked. Add the onions and thyme. Stir in the livers and cook for 2 to 3 minutes.

Remove the liver mixture from the frying pan using a slotted spoon. Place in a blender and purée with the cream, reserved Madeira, sherry, brandy, salt and pepper. Chill for 4 hours.

Serve with crackers.

Egg *and* Caviar Appetizer

Here is a recipe for egg salad with a gourmet difference. It is best served in a glass bowl to show off the colourful layers.

PREPARATION TIME: 15 minutes
YIELD: 8 servings

8 oz	cream cheese, room temperature	250 g
2-3 Tbsp	milk	25-45 mL
8	eggs, hard-boiled	8
1/4 cup	mayonnaise	50 mL
1 small	onion, chopped	1 small
2 1/2 oz	caviar	70 g
	parsley sprigs as garnish	

Beat the cream cheese with the milk until it is the consistency of sour cream. Finely chop the hard-boiled eggs and combine with the mayonnaise in a serving bowl. Sprinkle the eggs with the chopped onion. Spread the cream cheese on top using a wet knife. Spread caviar on top of the cream cheese. Garnish with parsley sprigs if desired.

Serve with pumpernickel bread.

Almond Cheese Ball

The crunchy almond coating and the subtly-flavoured interior combine to make a cheese ball that is out of the ordinary.

PREPARATION TIME: 20 minutes
COOKING TIME: 15 minutes
REFRIGERATION TIME: 1 hour
YIELD: 10 servings

1 cup	slivered almonds	250 mL
8 oz	cream cheese, room temperature	250 g
1/2 cup	mayonnaise	125 mL
5 strips	bacon, crisply cooked and crumbled	5 strips
1 Tbsp	chopped green onions	15 mL
1 tsp	caraway seeds	5 mL

Preheat the oven to 300°F (150°C).

Spread almonds in a shallow pan and bake for 10 to 15 minutes, stirring often, until they begin to turn colour.

Combine the cream cheese and mayonnaise. Add the bacon, onions and caraway seeds, blending well. Cover and chill for 1 hour. Form mixture into a ball and press almonds onto the surface.

Serve at room temperature with crackers or pumpernickel bread.

Barbecued Eggplant

Try this lemony eggplant instead of the traditional babaganoush.

PREPARATION TIME: 15 minutes
SITTING TIME: 30 minutes
COOKING TIME: 30-45 minutes
YIELD: 1 1/2 cups (375 mL)

1 large	eggplant	1 large
1 tsp	salt	5 mL
2 cloves	garlic, crushed	2 cloves
1/3-1/2 cup	olive oil	75-125 mL
	juice of 1 lemon	
	salt and pepper to taste	
	parsley as garnish	

Preheat the oven to broil or start barbecue.

Slice the eggplant in half lengthwise and sprinkle with salt. Cover with a paper towel and let sit at least 1/2 hour to remove the bitter juices. Rinse.

Place skin side up on a greased cookie sheet under the broiler, about 2 inches below the heating element, or skin side down on the hot barbecue. Cook until the skin is very charred and the eggplant flesh is soft. Cool until the eggplant can be handled.

Scoop out the flesh into a bowl and season with the garlic, olive oil, lemon juice, salt and pepper. Mash with a fork until the mixture is easily spread. Garnish with parsley.

Serve at room temperature with pita bread or crackers.

Curried Salmon Tarts

These warm, spicy tidbits have a way of disappearing rapidly.

PREPARATION TIME: **10 minutes**
COOKING TIME: **10 minutes**
YIELD: **18 small appetizers**

18 slices	white bread	18 slices
2 Tbsp	butter	25 mL
2 Tbsp	flour	25 mL
1 cup	milk	250 mL
1 can	red salmon, drained and	1 can
(7 1/2-oz)	flaked	(213 g)
1 Tbsp	curry powder	15 mL
pinch	pepper	pinch

Preheat the oven to broil.

Cut the crusts off the bread. Press down to flatten the slices. Gently push each slice into a large muffin tin to form a little cup. Place under the broiler, checking frequently, until toasted. Remove and cool.

Melt the butter in a saucepan set over low heat. Stir in the flour. Gradually stir in the milk and heat until thickened. Stir in the salmon, curry powder and pepper.

Spoon the hot salmon mixture into the toasted cups. Arrange on a tray and serve immediately.

Smoked Salmon Rolls

Smoked salmon and cream cheese are always a special combination. When prepared in this innovative manner, they make a delectable appetizer.

PREPARATION TIME: **20** minutes
REFRIGERATION TIME: **1** hour
YIELD: **32-40** rolls

8 oz	cream cheese	250 g
1/4 cup	mayonnaise	50 mL
2 Tbsp	chopped fresh dill	25 mL
dash	freshly ground pepper	dash
1 lb	smoked salmon, sliced	500 g
	juice of 1 lemon	

Combine the cream cheese, mayonnaise, dill and pepper. Spread a thin layer of the cheese mixture on each slice of salmon. Roll tightly and wrap in waxed paper. Refrigerate for 1 hour.

Remove the paper and cut each roll into bite-size rounds. Secure each piece with a toothpick or a cocktail stick. Sprinkle with lemon juice.

Serve with slices of pumpernickel bread.

Crispy Cheese Cubes

Jazzy triple-decker sandwiches make a great appetizer for an informal dinner or a substantial lunch dish when served whole.

PREPARATION TIME: **10 minutes**
COOKING TIME: **10 minutes**
YIELD: **4 servings**

6 slices	white bread, crusts removed	6 slices
1/4 cup	butter, room temperature	50 mL
1/4 cup	grated Parmesan cheese	50 mL
2	eggs	2
1/4 cup	milk	50 mL
pinch	basil	pinch
5 drops	Tabasco sauce	5 drops
4 drops	Worcestershire sauce	4 drops
1/2 tsp	salt	2 mL
1 tsp	garlic powder	5 mL

Preheat the oven to 400°F (200°C).

Generously butter both sides of 4 slices of bread and sprinkle with Parmesan cheese.

Combine the eggs, milk, basil, Tabasco, Worcestershire, salt and garlic powder. Dip the remaining slices of bread in this mixture.

Place 2 of the buttered bread slices on a cookie sheet. Stack the dipped slices on top and then top these with the remaining 2 buttered pieces.

Bake for 5 minutes, then turn on the broiler and broil until golden on top.

Cut the sandwiches into 1-inch (2.5 cm) cubes. Spear with toothpicks and serve immediately.

Cheese Crispies

Both variations of these 'can't-eat-just-one' appetizers will have your company guessing at the secret crunchy ingredient.

PREPARATION TIME: 30 minutes
REFRIGERATION TIME: 1 hour
COOKING TIME: 10-20 minutes
YIELD: 4 dozen

Basic Ingredients

1 cup	butter, room temperature	250 mL
1-1 1/2 cups	all-purpose flour*	250-275 mL
4 cups	crisp rice cereal	1 L
pinch	salt	pinch

Spicy Crispies

2 cups	grated old Cheddar cheese	500 mL
1/4 tsp	Tabasco sauce	1 mL
1/4 tsp	Worcestershire sauce	1 mL
pinch	cayenne pepper	pinch

Savoury Crispies

1 1/2 cups	grated Swiss cheese	375 mL
1/2 cup	grated smoked Gruyère cheese	125 mL
1 tsp	dill	5 mL
1 tsp	parsley	5 mL
1 Tbsp	finely chopped onion	15 mL

Preheat the oven to 350°F (180°C).

Cream together the butter and the ingredients for either the spicy or savoury Crispies. Stir in the flour, cereal and salt. (Using your hands makes it easier to combine the mixture.)

Roll the dough into logs 1 1/2 inches (4 cm) in diameter, 6 inches (15 cm) long. Wrap in waxed paper and chill for 1 hour.

Remove from the refrigerator and unwrap. Using a knife dipped in cold water, carefully cut into rounds 1/4-inch (5 mm) thick. Place on a lightly greased cookie sheet, leaving enough room between the Crispies for spreading. Bake for 10 to 20 minutes (less time for less flour and thinner rounds), until lightly browned.

*The texture is altered by the quantity of flour. For a crisp, thin Crispie use less flour. For a softer, more 'biscuit-like' Crispie, use more flour.

Cheese Straws

Your guests will snap up this tangy finger food at your next cocktail party.

PREPARATION TIME: 25 minutes
COOKING TIME: 15-20 minutes
YIELD: 6 dozen

8 oz	extra-sharp Cheddar cheese, grated	250 g
1/2 cup	butter, room temperature	125 mL
1/2 tsp	salt	2 mL
dash	cayenne pepper	dash
1 1/2 cups	all-purpose flour	375 mL
1/4 tsp	paprika	1 mL

Preheat the oven to 350°F (180°C).

Combine all of the ingredients to make a soft dough.

Roll out the dough onto a floured board until 1/4 inch (5 mm) thick. Cut into strips 3 inches (7.5 cm) long and 1/2 inch (1 cm) wide.

Place the strips on two ungreased shiny cookie sheets. Bake for 15 to 20 minutes. Cut the strips into 2-inch (5 cm) pieces while still warm. Let cool on the pans. Sprinkle lightly with paprika.

Store in an airtight container.

Zesty Super Nachos

Our nachos are as good as those found in any Mexican restaurant.

PREPARATION TIME: 15 minutes
COOKING TIME: 3-5 minutes
YIELD: 20-24 nachos

1 large	avocado, mashed	1 large
	juice of 1/2 lemon	
2 cloves	garlic, minced	2 cloves
	salt to taste	
1 box (7-oz)	nacho chips	1 box (198 g)
1/2	green pepper, diced	1/2
1	tomato, diced	1
10	black olives, sliced	10
10	green olives, sliced	10
1 1/2 cups	Monterey Jack cheese, grated	375 mL
1 jar (10 1/4-oz)	jalapeño peppers, sliced	1 jar (290 g)
1 cup	sour cream	250 mL
1 jar (8-oz)	Mexican hot sauce	1 jar (227 mL)

Preheat the oven to broil.

Combine the avocado, lemon juice, garlic and salt in a bowl to make guacamole. Set aside.

Place the nacho chips on an ovenproof tray. Mix together the green pepper, tomato, black and green olives. Put 3/4 of this mixture on top of the nacho chips. Sprinkle with the cheese. Cover with the remainder of the vegetable mixture. Top each nacho with a slice of jalapeño pepper.

Broil the nachos until the cheese is melted, about 3 to 5 minutes.

To serve, place the nachos on a serving platter. Surround with bowls of the guacamole, sour cream and hot sauce.

Stuffed Artichoke Bottoms

This delightful 'party-pack' recipe makes six of the red ones, half a dozen of the green ones. They go well with good wine and conversation.

PREPARATION TIME: **30** minutes
YIELD: **12** large appetizers

2 Tbsp	butter	25 mL
1 large	onion, diced	1 large
8 oz	cream cheese, room	250 g
	temperature	
1/4 cup	sour cream	50 mL
2 slices	smoked salmon, shredded	2 slices
2 cans	artichoke bottoms,	2 cans
(14-oz)	rinsed and drained	(398 mL)
2	scallions, thinly sliced	2
2 tsp	red caviar	10 mL

Heat the butter in a small frying pan. Sauté the onion until soft. Combine with half of the cream cheese. Combine the remaining cream cheese with the sour cream and salmon.

Pat the artichoke bottoms dry. Fill half of them with the onion and cheese mixture. Top with the scallions. Fill the remaining artichoke bottoms with the salmon and cheese mixture and top with the caviar.

Arrange attractively on a serving tray and pass around.

Potato Wedges

Quick and easy to prepare, this appetizer is also delicious as a snack food. It will be devoured by adults and children alike.

PREPARATION TIME: 10 minutes
COOKING TIME: 15 minutes
YIELD: 4 servings

3 medium	potatoes, cut into wedges lengthwise	3 medium
	vegetable oil	
	seasoned salt	
3/4 cup	sour cream	175 mL
1/3 cup	shredded Cheddar cheese	75 mL

Preheat the oven to broil.

Place potato wedges, cut sides down, on a rack in a greased broiler pan. Brush with oil and sprinkle with seasoned salt. Broil until brown, about 5 minutes. Turn and brush the other side with oil. Sprinkle with seasoned salt. Broil until tender, about 10 more minutes.

Spoon the sour cream into the centre of a large serving platter and sprinkle with the cheese. Arrange the potato wedges around the sour cream.

Variation: Try these with oregano, steak spice, paprika, Italian seasoning or any other seasoning for a different taste sensation.

Bacon-Wrapped Water Chestnuts

This Oriental delight provides an unusual blend of tastes and textures.

MARINATING TIME: **4 hours**
PREPARATION TIME: **15 minutes**
COOKING TIME: **20 minutes**
YIELD: **40**

1/2 cup	soy sauce	125 mL
2 tsp	ginger	10 mL
1 can	water chestnuts	1 can
(8-oz)		(227 mL)
3/4 cup	sugar	175 mL
1/2 lb	bacon, sliced	250 g

Mix the soy sauce and ginger together. Add the water chestnuts and refrigerate for four hours.

Remove the chestnuts from the marinade with a slotted spoon and shake off the excess moisture. Roll in the sugar. Cut the bacon into thirds. Wrap each chestnut in bacon and secure with toothpicks.

Place the chestnuts on a broiler pan and broil on both sides until the bacon is done.

Zucchini-Cheese Slices

Those who sampled this dish proclaimed it simply delicious.

PREPARATION TIME: 15 minutes
COOKING TIME: 5-7 minutes
YIELD: 16 pieces

1	zucchini	1
1/2 cup	mayonnaise	125 mL
2 Tbsp	grated onion	25 mL
2 (8-in)	French rolls	2 (20 cm)
1 cup	grated Gruyère cheese	250 mL

Preheat the oven to broil.

Grate the unpeeled zucchini and squeeze out the excess moisture. Stir in the mayonnaise and the onion.

Cut each roll into 8 slices and spread with the zucchini mixture. Top with the grated cheese and broil until golden, about 5 to 7 minutes.

Zucchini Hors d'Oeuvres

This one-step dish works equally well for the brunch crowd.

PREPARATION TIME: 20 minutes
COOKING TIME: 25 minutes
YIELD: 30 hors d'oeuvres

1 cup	biscuit mix	250 mL
1/2 cup	finely chopped onion	125 mL
1 cup	grated Cheddar cheese	250 mL
2 Tbsp	finely chopped fresh parsley	25 mL
1/2 tsp	salt	2 mL
dash	pepper	dash
1/2 tsp	oregano	2 mL
1 large clove	garlic, minced	1 large clove
1/2 cup	vegetable oil	125 mL
4	eggs, lightly beaten	4
3 small	zucchini, grated	3 small
	paprika	

Preheat the oven to 350°F (180°C).

Combine all the ingredients. Pour into a greased 9-by-13 inch (4 L) baking dish. Sprinkle with paprika. Bake for 25 minutes.

Cool slightly prior to serving. Cut into squares and serve in paper muffin cups.

Oysters au Gratin

Such an attractive and elegant appetizer justifies the trip to the fish store for fresh oysters.

PREPARATION TIME: **40 minutes**
COOKING TIME: **3-5 minutes**
YIELD: **4 servings**

2 Tbsp	grated Parmesan cheese	25 mL
1/2 cup	grated Emmenthal cheese	125 mL
3 Tbsp	bread crumbs	45 mL
3 Tbsp	butter, room temperature	45 mL
pinch	minced chives	pinch
pinch	tarragon	pinch
pinch	garlic powder	pinch
1 Tbsp	dry sherry	15 mL
12	fresh oysters, shucked	12
3-4 tsp	oyster liquor	15-20 mL

Preheat the oven to broil.

Combine the Parmesan and Emmenthal cheese with the bread crumbs.

Combine the butter, chives, tarragon, garlic powder and sherry.

Place 3 oysters and 1 teaspoon (5 mL) of oyster liquor in each of 4 scallop baking shells. Dot the seasoned butter on top of the oysters. Cover with the cheese mixture.

Broil on a baking sheet for 3 to 5 minutes, until crispy and golden brown.

Shrimp-and-Grapefruit Cocktail

This elegant starter combines an eclectic mix of ingredients. The result is sensational.

PREPARATION TIME: 30 minutes
YIELD: 4 servings

3	grapefruit	3

Mayonnaise

1 1/2 tsp	Dijon mustard	7 mL
1	egg yolk, room temperature	1
3/4 cup	vegetable oil	175 mL
1 tsp	vinegar or lemon juice	5 mL
1 1/2 tsp	ketchup	7 mL
1/2 tsp	Tabasco sauce	2 mL
	salt and pepper to taste	
7 oz	baby shrimp, cooked and drained	198 g

Halve the grapefruit and remove the segments with a teaspoon. Discard the membrane. Reserve the shells and drain, cut side down, in a colander. Dry the grapefruit sections on paper towel.

Mayonnaise: Combine the mustard and egg yolk. Slowly add the oil, drop by drop, beating constantly. When the mayonnaise is thick, stir in the vinegar or lemon juice and the ketchup, Tabasco, salt and pepper.

To serve, combine the grapefruit sections, mayonnaise and shrimp. Spoon into the grapefruit shells.

Smoked Trout with Horseradish Sauce

Try this appetizer for an impressive beginning to a sit-down dinner party.

PREPARATION TIME: **20 minutes**
YIELD: **4 servings**

2 whole	smoked brook trout	2 whole
1/2 cup	35% cream	125 mL
3 Tbsp	prepared horseradish	45 mL
4	leaves romaine lettuce	4
	parsley or dill sprigs as garnish	
	lemon slices as garnish	

Skin the trout and remove the heads and tails. Carefully fillet the trout, removing all the bones.

Whip the cream until stiff peaks form. Fold in the horseradish.

To serve, place a leaf of romaine lettuce on each plate. Arrange the trout fillet on top. Garnish with the parsley or dill sprigs and lemon slices. Serve the horseradish sauce on the side.

Warren's Amazing Szechuan Noodles

A spicy first course, this dish is also a treat as leftovers.

PREPARATION TIME: 10 minutes
COOKING TIME: 3-5 minutes
YIELD: 4-6 servings

Noodles

1 lb	Chinese Rice Stick Noodles* (vermicelli)	500 g
1 Tbsp	sesame oil*	15 mL

Sauce

3/4 cup	Chinese-style barbecue sauce*	175 mL
2 Tbsp	sesame oil*	25 mL
1 tsp	Chinese hot sauce*	5 mL
3 Tbsp	Hoisin sauce*	45 mL
2 Tbsp	soy sauce	25 mL
1/3 cup	crunchy peanut butter	75 mL

Topping

3	chopped green onions	3

Noodles: Cook the noodles in boiling water until soft, 3 to 5 minutes. Rinse well under cold water to remove starch. Place in a large bowl and stir in the sesame oil.

Sauce: Combine all the sauce ingredients and pour over the noodles. Mix well.

Topping: Sprinkle the green onions on top of the noodles.

*Available in Oriental food stores.

SOUPS

Avocado-Crab Soup

We know your guests will appreciate the striking colour combinations in this soup.

PREPARATION TIME: 15 minutes
REFRIGERATION TIME: 4 hours
YIELD: 3-4 servings

2 ripe	avocados	2 ripe
1 cup	chicken broth	250 mL
1/2 tsp	curry powder	2 mL
1 Tbsp	lemon juice	15 mL
	white pepper to taste	
1/2 cup	flaked crab meat	125 mL
2 Tbsp	sliced almonds	25 mL

Peel the avocados and cut into chunks. Combine with the chicken broth, curry powder, lemon juice and pepper and purée in a blender until smooth. Refrigerate for 4 hours.

One-half hour prior to serving, add the crab meat and almonds. If the soup is too thick, thin with a little milk, cream or yogurt.

Serve cold.

Cold Borscht Soup

On a hot summer's day, try this refreshing soup to cool off.

PREPARATION TIME: 15 minutes
REFRIGERATION TIME: 1 hour
YIELD: 8 servings

2 cans (19-oz)	whole beets	2 cans (540 mL)
1 pt	sour cream	500 mL
1	egg, hard-boiled and chopped	1
1 cup	peeled and chopped cucumber	250 mL
2-3	green onions, chopped	2-3
1 tsp	salt	5 mL
1 1/2 Tbsp	chopped fresh dill	20 mL
4 cups	water	1 L

Drain the beets, reserving the liquid in a large serving bowl. Grate the beets into the bowl. Add the sour cream, mixing until smooth. Stir in the egg, cucumber, onions, salt and dill. Mix until well blended. Add the water, stirring constantly until it becomes smooth and is the desired consistency. Chill in the refrigerator until cold, for about 1 hour.

This soup keeps well in the refrigerator.

Curried Carrot Soup

This is a delicate, colourful soup, flavourful in a subtle way.

PREPARATION TIME: **10 minutes**
COOKING TIME: **25 minutes**
YIELD: **6 servings**

1/4 cup	butter	50 mL
1 medium	onion, chopped	1 medium
1 tsp	curry powder	5 mL
8 large	carrots, peeled and sliced	8 large
4	chicken bouillon cubes	4
6 cups	water	1.5 L
dash	nutmeg	dash
3 Tbsp	sherry	45 mL
	salt and pepper to taste	
	chives as garnish	

Melt the butter in a large saucepan. Sauté the onion and curry powder until soft. Add the remaining ingredients except the chives and bring to a boil. Simmer until the carrots are tender, about 20 minutes. Purée the soup in a blender, processor or food mill. Return to saucepan and heat through.

Garnish with chopped chives and serve immediately.

Healthy Carrot Potage

Provide a hearty beginning to an autumn dinner with this simple but delicious soup.

PREPARATION TIME: **15 minutes**
COOKING TIME: **25 minutes**
YIELD: **6-8 servings**

3 cups	water	750 mL
3 cups	chicken bouillon	750 mL
6 medium	carrots, sliced	6 medium
1	onion, chopped	1
2 stalks	celery, diced	2 stalks
2 medium	potatoes, diced	2 medium
1 tsp	coriander	5 mL
1 cup	milk	250 mL
1/2 cup	18% cream	125 mL
	salt and pepper to taste	
	fresh chopped chives or parsley as garnish	

Combine the water and bouillon in a large saucepan. Add the carrots, onion, celery, potatoes and coriander. Cook until the vegetables are tender, approximately 20 minutes.

Purée the soup in a blender until smooth. Return to the saucepan. Add the milk and cream. Season to taste with the salt and pepper. Heat through.

Serve garnished with chives or parsley.

Triple 'C' Soup

The three main components of this soup—celery, cream and cauliflower—combine to make a pretty and elegant soup.

PREPARATION TIME: 10 minutes
COOKING TIME: 15 minutes
YIELD: 4 servings

1 medium	onion	1 medium
4	celery stalks	4
1/2	cauliflower	1/2
1/2 cup	unsalted butter	125 mL
1/3 cup	flour	75 mL
4 cups	chicken stock	1 L
1 cup	35% cream	250 mL
	salt and pepper to taste	
	parsley as garnish	

Coarsely chop the onion, celery and cauliflower. Sauté in the butter until the onions are translucent.

Purée the vegetables in a food processor, blender or food mill and turn into a saucepan. Add the flour and mix completely.

Add the stock and bring to a boil. Remove from the heat and stir in the cream. Add salt and pepper to taste.

Serve with a sprinkling of parsley.

Cream of Leek Soup
with Stilton

Our version of this soup is not as rich as most because milk and chicken stock replace the traditional heavy cream—fewer calories and more taste!

PREPARATION TIME: 15 minutes
COOKING TIME: 30 minutes
YIELD: 4 servings

1 Tbsp	butter	15 mL
1	shallot, finely chopped	1
2 medium	leeks, washed and chopped	2 medium
2 medium	potatoes, peeled and diced	2 medium
2 1/2 cups	light chicken stock, hot	625 mL
1/4 cup	35% cream	50 mL
1/2 cup	2% milk	125 mL
	salt to taste	
	freshly ground black pepper to taste	
	freshly ground nutmeg to taste	
	lemon juice to taste	
2 oz	Stilton cheese, crumbled	55 g

Melt the butter in a deep pan. Add the shallot and leeks. Cover and sweat over low heat until translucent. Add the potatoes and chicken stock. Cook briskly until the potatoes are cooked. Cool and add enough water to equal 3 cups (750 mL) of liquid. Purée roughly in blender or food processor.

Combine cream and milk in a separate pan. Boil for 2 minutes. Add puréed vegetable mixture and return to a boil. Add the salt, pepper, nutmeg and lemon juice. Pour into heated soup bowls and sprinkle with crumbled Stilton cheese.

Hearty Spinach Soup

If you enjoy spinach, then this substantial soup is for you. The flavour is rich—just like mother used to make.

PREPARATION TIME: **20 minutes**
COOKING TIME: **35 minutes**
YIELD: **4-6 servings**

1	onion, finely chopped	1
3 Tbsp	cracked or pearl barley	45 mL
2 qts	beef stock	2 L
1 pkg	frozen spinach, chopped	1 pkg
(10 1/2-oz)		(300 g)
or 10 oz	fresh spinach	*or* 283 g
1 Tbsp	chopped fresh parsley	15 mL
1 Tbsp	chopped fresh dill	15 mL
1 slice	lemon, rind removed	1 slice
	salt and pepper to taste	
2	potatoes, diced	2
1 Tbsp	lemon juice	15 mL
1	egg, hard-boiled and sliced	1
	as garnish	
	sour cream as garnish	

Cook the onion and the barley in 1/3 of the liquid until the barley is tender. Add the remaining liquid, spinach, parsley, dill, lemon slice, salt and pepper. Bring to the boil and add the potatoes. Simmer until the potatoes are tender. Add lemon juice. Taste and adjust seasoning if desired.

Garnish with egg rounds and sour cream to taste. This soup may be enjoyed hot or cold. Served with fresh bread, it is a meal in itself.

Cream of Tomato Soup

Surprisingly good given its easy preparation, this soup is particularly suitable as a first course because it is not too filling.

PREPARATION TIME: **10 minutes**
COOKING TIME: **40 minutes**
YIELD: **6-8 servings**

8 cups	water	2 L
3	chicken bouillon cubes	3
1 large	onion, chopped	1 large
10 medium	tomatoes, peeled and chopped	10 medium
2 cups	chopped celery	500 mL
1 tsp	salt	5 mL
3 Tbsp	honey	45 mL
2 Tbsp	butter	25 mL
1 tsp	paprika	5 mL
2 cups	10% cream	500 mL

Bring the water to a boil in a large saucepan. Add the bouillon cubes, onion, tomatoes, celery and salt. Cover and simmer for 30 minutes. Transfer to a blender or food processor and purée until smooth. Return to the pan. Add the honey, butter and paprika. Set over very low heat, add the cream slowly and cook until heated through.

Note: When fresh tomatoes are not available, canned plum tomatoes may be substituted. A 28-ounce (796 mL) can is appropriate. Substitute the juice from the can for an equivalent amount of water.

Herbed Tomato Soup

The unusual blend of herbs makes an extra special tomato soup.

PREPARATION TIME: 15 minutes
COOKING TIME: 45 minutes
YIELD: 6 servings

1/2 cup	butter	125 mL
2 Tbsp	olive oil	25 mL
1 large	onion, thinly sliced	1 large
1 tsp	fresh thyme	5 mL
1 tsp	fresh basil	5 mL
1 tsp	fresh oregano	5 mL
1 tsp	fresh dill	5 mL
1 can (28-oz)	Italian plum tomatoes	1 can (796 mL)
1 can (15-oz)	Italian plum tomatoes	1 can (426 mL)
3 Tbsp	tomato paste	45 mL
1/4 cup	flour	50 mL
3 3/4 cups	chicken stock	925 mL
	sugar to taste	
	salt to taste	
	white pepper to taste	
	sour cream or yogurt as garnish	

Combine the butter, oil, onion, thyme, basil, oregano and dill in a large saucepan. Cook over medium-low heat, stirring occasionally, until the onion is soft and golden.

Drain the tomatoes. Add the tomatoes and tomato paste to the onions. Simmer uncovered for 10 minutes, stirring often.

In a small bowl, blend the flour and 1/2 cup (125 mL) chicken stock. Add it to the tomato mixture. Add the remaining stock and heat on high until just below the boiling point. Simmer uncovered for 25 minutes, stirring frequently. Remove the soup in batches to a blender and purée. Add the sugar, salt and pepper. Pour into heated soup bowls. Garnish with sour cream or yogurt.

Harvest Soup

The bounty of harvest vegetables is used to its best in a colourful soup.

PREPARATION TIME: 15 minutes
COOKING TIME: 45 minutes
YIELD: 4-6 servings

9 cups	beef stock or bouillon	2.25 L
1 medium	onion, chopped	1 medium
3 Tbsp	butter	45 mL
1	bay leaf	1
4	peppercorns	4
1 can (14-oz)	whole beets	1 can (540 mL)
1/2 small	cabbage, shredded	1/2 small
2	carrots, diced	2
2	celery stalks, diced	2
1 Tbsp	lemon juice	15 mL
1 Tbsp	chopped fresh dill or 1 1/2 tsp (7 mL) dried	15 mL
	salt to taste	
1/4 cup	sour cream	50 mL
	chopped dill pickles as garnish	

Prepare stock or bouillon. Sauté the onion in the butter in a large pot until transparent. Add the stock, bay leaf and peppercorns. Simmer for 15 minutes. Add the beets, cabbage, carrots, celery and lemon juice. Cook, covered, for 30 minutes. Season the soup with dill and salt.

Garnish each serving with a dollop of sour cream and chopped pickles.

Italian Vegetable Soup

This unique version of vegetable soup needs only the addition of garlic bread to round out the meal.

PREPARATION TIME: 15 minutes
COOKING TIME: 25 minutes
YIELD: 8 servings

1 lb	Italian sausage	500 g
1 medium	onion, sliced	1 medium
1 can (16-oz)	whole tomatoes	1 can (454 mL)
1 can (15-oz)	garbanzo beans, drained	1 can (426 ml)
1 can (10 1/2-oz)	condensed beef broth	1 can (300 mL)
1 1/2 cups	water	375 mL
2 medium	zucchini, sliced	2 medium
1/2 tsp	basil	2 mL
	grated Parmesan cheese	

Sauté the sausage and onion in a large saucepan until sausage is light brown. Drain. Add the tomatoes (with liquid), beans, broth, water, zucchini and basil. Break up the tomatoes. Heat to boiling, then reduce heat. Cover and simmer until zucchini is tender, about 5 minutes.

Sprinkle with cheese.

Middle Eastern Vegetable Soup

If you like your food hot and spicy, we suggest the following for a cold winter's evening.

PREPARATION TIME: 20 minutes
COOKING TIME: 20 minutes
YIELD: 6 servings

6 cups	chicken or vegetable stock	1.5 L
2 medium	potatoes, sliced	2 medium
2 medium	carrots, sliced diagonally	2 medium
1 large stalk	celery, sliced	1 large stalk
1 large	onion, sliced	1 large
1 cup	okra, trimmed	250 mL
1 medium	zucchini, sliced	1 medium
1 cup	spinach	250 mL
2 large	tomatoes, cut in eighths	2 large
1 handful	fresh parsley, chopped	1 handful
2-3 Tbsp	tomato paste	25-45 mL
2 Tbsp	chopped fresh ginger root	25 mL
3 cloves	garlic, crushed	3 cloves
4-5	dried red chilies, crumbled	4-5
1 tsp	ground cumin	5 mL

Bring the stock to a boil in a large saucepan. Add the potatoes, carrots, celery, onion, okra, zucchini, spinach, tomatoes, parsley and tomato paste. When the stock has returned to a boil, reduce the heat to simmer. Add the ginger, garlic, chilies and cumin. Cover and simmer for approximately 20 minutes.

Zucchini Cream Soup

Serve this summer soup hot or cold.

PREPARATION TIME: 20 minutes
COOKING TIME: 10 minutes
YIELD: 6 servings

2 lb	young zucchini, diced	1 kg
1 cup	boiling water	250 mL
1 tsp	salt	5 mL
2 cups	milk	500 mL
1 cup	chopped onion	250 mL
1/2 clove	garlic, minced	1/2 clove
2 Tbsp	butter	25 mL
2 cups	10% cream	500 mL
1 tsp	sugar	5 mL
	salt to taste	
	pepper to taste	
	sour cream or yogurt as garnish	

Place the zucchini in a saucepan and cover with the water and salt. Bring to a boil. Cover and simmer until tender. Remove pan from heat and add the milk.

In a separate pan, sauté the onion and garlic in the butter until tender.

Purée the zucchini and onion mixtures in a blender until smooth. Return to pan. Add the cream, sugar, salt and pepper. Heat through or chill.

Garnish with sour cream or yogurt.

Note: If the zucchini is mature, it should be peeled to prevent a bitter taste.

One-Pot Zucchini Soup

Rich in flavour but not in calories, this deep green soup is out of the ordinary. The bonus is that it can be served to people with a dairy or wheat allergy.

PREPARATION TIME: **30 minutes**
COOKING TIME: **30 minutes**
YIELD: **8 servings**

2 Tbsp	oil	25 mL
1	onion, chopped	1
1 stalk	celery, sliced	1 stalk
3	zucchini, sliced	3
2 cloves	garlic, minced	2 cloves
4 tsp	curry powder	20 mL
6 cups	chicken stock	1.5 L
2	potatoes, peeled and diced	2
1/2 cup	parsley, chopped	125 mL
	salt and pepper to taste	
	yogurt as garnish (optional)	

In a large pot, sauté the onion in the oil. Add the celery, zucchini, garlic, and curry powder. When the vegetables are soft, add the chicken stock, potatoes and parsley. Cover and simmer for 30 minutes. Season to taste. When cool, purée in a food processor or blender. Return to the pot. Heat and serve.

Serve with a dollop of plain yogurt if desired.

MAIN DISHES

Seduction Chicken

The seductive flavour of this saucy chicken is a knockout.

PREPARATION TIME: 15 minutes
COOKING TIME: 45 minutes
YIELD: 6 servings

1/4 cup	butter	50 mL
1 can	sliced peaches	1 can
(14-oz)		(398 mL)
1 can	apricot halves	1 can
(14-oz)		(398 mL)
1 small	onion, chopped	1 small
1/4 cup	honey	50 mL
2 tsp	Dijon mustard	10 mL
1 1/2 tsp	curry powder	7 mL
1 1/2 tsp	ground ginger	7 mL
	salt and pepper to taste	
6 pieces	chicken, breasts or legs	6 pieces
2 tsp	sesame seeds, toasted	10 mL
	(optional)	

Preheat the oven to 375°F (190°C).

Place the butter in a 9-by-13 inch (4 L) pan and set in the oven for 5 minutes, until melted. Drain the peaches and apricots, reserving the liquid. Purée the peaches, apricots, onion, honey, mustard and spices. Add a little of the reserved liquid if the mixture is too thick. (It should resemble a runny apple-sauce.) Add the mixture to the melted butter in the pan and return to the oven for about 5 minutes, or until bubbly.

Place the chicken pieces in the sauce, skin side down. Bake for 30 minutes, basting every 10 minutes. Turn and sprinkle with the sesame seeds. Baste. Bake for 15 minutes or until golden brown.

The extra sauce may be spooned over rice.

Parmesan Chicken Breasts

This fragrant chicken is redolent of herbs.

PREPARATION TIME: **20 minutes**
COOKING TIME: **35-40 minutes**
YIELD: **8 servings**

3/4 cup	butter	175 mL
1-2 cloves	garlic, crushed	1-2 cloves
1 1/2 tsp	Dijon mustard	7 mL
1/2 tsp	Worcestershire sauce	2 mL
2 cups	fresh bread crumbs	500 mL
1 cup	freshly grated Parmesan cheese	250 mL
	salt and pepper to taste	
2 Tbsp	chopped fresh parsley	25 mL
2 Tbsp	chopped fresh basil	25 mL
or 1 Tbsp	dried basil	*or* 15 mL
4 whole	chicken breasts, boned, skinned and halved	4 whole

Preheat the oven to 350°F (180°C).

Melt the butter in a small saucepan and add the garlic, mustard and Worcestershire sauce. Remove from the heat and allow to cool to lukewarm. In a shallow pan combine the bread crumbs, cheese, salt, pepper, parsley and basil.

Pat the chicken breasts dry. Dip each piece in the butter and then roll in the bread-crumb mixture, patting to coat completely. Arrange in a 9-by-13 inch (4 L) shallow baking pan and drizzle with the remaining butter.

Bake 35 to 40 minutes until golden brown, basting after about 20 minutes.

Chicken Breasts with Goat Cheese and Basil

Be sure to use domestic goat cheese as the imported variety is too strong and overwhelms the delicate flavour of the basil.

PREPARATION TIME: **20 minutes**
COOKING TIME: **25 minutes**
YIELD: **4 servings**

2	chicken breasts, boned and halved, with skin intact	2
4 oz	mild goat cheese	125 g
40	fresh basil leaves	40
	olive oil	
2	green onions, finely chopped	2
1/4 cup	chicken stock	50 mL
3/4 cup	35% cream	175 mL
	salt and freshly ground pepper to taste	

Cut a pocket approximately 1-by-2 inches (2.5 × 5 cm) in the thickest part of each chicken breast half. For each breast, wrap one-quarter of the cheese in 3 or 4 basil leaves. Place the wrapped cheese in the pocket, gently closing the opening. Do *not* use toothpicks or skewers to close. Place 2 basil leaves *under* the skin on the top side of each chicken breast.

Pour a thin layer of olive oil into a frying pan. Sauté the chicken breasts over moderate heat, 6 to 10 minutes each side. Keep the chicken warm.

To prepare the sauce, simmer the onion in the stock and cream until reduced to 1/3 cup (75 mL). Strain.

To serve, cut the remaining basil leaves in julienne strips and stir half into the sauce. Cut each chicken breast into 1/3- to 1/2-inch (8 to 12.5 mm) slices. Divide the sauce evenly over the four plates. Arrange the chicken slices in an overlapping manner on top of the sauce. Garnish with the remaining julienned basil.

Serve with asparagus and a light French stick.

Note: The chicken may also be served at room temperature or chilled on a bed of mixed greens. It may also be barbecued approximately 3 to 5 minutes per side.

Tarragon Chicken Flambé

The addition of Madeira or cognac makes an unusual tarragon chicken.

PREPARATION TIME: **5 minutes**
COOKING TIME: **20 minutes**
YIELD: **4 servings**

1/4 cup	flour	50 mL
	salt and freshly ground pepper to taste	
4 half	chicken breasts, skinned and boned	4 half
2 Tbsp	butter	25 mL
1/4 cup	Madeira or cognac	50 mL
1/2 cup	35% cream	125 mL
1 1/2 tsp	dried tarragon	7 mL

Combine the flour, salt and pepper in a shallow dish. Roll the chicken breasts in the mixture to cover lightly.

Melt the butter in a frying pan. Sauté the chicken until lightly browned. Pour off any excess butter. Add the Madeira or cognac and ignite. When the flame has extinguished, stir in the cream and tarragon. Simmer until the sauce thickens, about 15 minutes.

Serve with rice and a green salad.

Szechuan Chicken and Peanuts

We love the combination of chicken, peanuts and Chinese sauces.

PREPARATION TIME: 30 minutes
COOKING TIME: 15 minutes
YIELD: 4 servings

1	egg	1
1 Tbsp	cornstarch	15 mL
1 Tbsp	soy sauce	15 mL
1 Tbsp	dry sherry	15 mL
2 whole	chicken breasts, boned and diced	2 whole
2 Tbsp	Hoisin sauce*	25 mL
1 Tbsp	plum sauce*	15 mL
1 tsp	chili paste*	5 mL
2 tsp	sugar	10 mL
3 Tbsp	peanut oil	45 mL
1/2 cup	water chestnuts	125 mL
1/2 cup	diced celery	125 mL
1/2 cup	roasted peanuts	125 mL

Combine the egg, cornstarch, soy sauce and sherry in a large bowl. Marinate the chicken in this mixture and let stand uncovered for 20 minutes.

Combine the Hoisin sauce, plum sauce, chili paste and sugar in a small bowl. Set this aside.

Put the oil in a heated wok or frying pan and heat the oil to the smoking point. Drain the chicken and add to the wok. Stir-fry until the chicken is no longer pink. Remove the chicken from the wok.

Add the water chestnuts and celery to the wok and stir-fry. Push the vegetables up the sides of the wok. Add the sauce mixture to the centre of the wok and bring to a boil. Stir down the vegetables, add the chicken and mix well. Add the peanuts and stir-fry for 1 minute. Serve with rice.

*Available in Oriental food stores.

Chicken in Black Bean Sauce

The pungent and aromatic flavour of black beans makes a surefire Oriental hit.

PREPARATION TIME: 30 minutes
COOKING TIME: 30 minutes
YIELD: 4 servings

4 tsp	black beans*	20 mL
2-3 lb	frying chicken	1-1.5 kg
2 Tbsp	oil	25 mL
3-4 cloves	garlic, minced	3-4 cloves
1 1/2 cups	chicken broth	375 mL
1 tsp	sugar	5 mL
2 Tbsp	cornstarch	25 mL
1/4 cup	soy sauce	50 mL
1/4 cup	chopped green onions	50 mL

Soak the black beans in boiling water to cover for 10 minutes. Cut the chicken into walnut-size pieces. Drain and finely chop the beans.

Heat oil in a wok or large frying pan. Add the garlic and beans. When the garlic turns golden, add the chicken and brown over high heat, tossing frequently. Add the chicken broth and sugar. Bring to a boil, then cover and simmer for 20 minutes.

Combine the cornstarch and soy sauce. Add to the chicken. Simmer until the sauce is thickened. Add the green onions.

Serve over rice.

*Available in Oriental food stores.

Lemon Chicken

The wonderful blend of textures and colours creates a magnificent chicken entrée for company or a buffet table.

PREPARATION TIME: **20 minutes**
COOKING TIME: **20 minutes**
YIELD: **6 servings**

1	egg white	1
2 tsp	vegetable oil	10 mL
3 whole	chicken breasts, boned, skinned and halved	3 whole
1/2 cup	flour	125 mL
	oil for frying	
3/4 cup	white sugar	175 mL
2 Tbsp	cornstarch	25 mL
1/2 cup	white wine vinegar	125 mL
2 tsp	grated lemon rind	10 mL
2 Tbsp	lemon juice	25 mL
1/4 cup	chicken broth	50 mL
1	red pepper, cut into strips	1
1	green pepper, cut into strips	1
1	carrot, cut into strips	1
3	green onions, cut into 1-inch (2.5 cm) lengths	3
1 can (10-oz)	mandarin oranges, drained	1 can (284 mL)
1 can (14-oz)	pineapple chunks, drained	1 can (398 mL)

Preheat the oven to 350°F (180°C).

Combine the egg white and 2 teaspoons (10 mL) oil in a medium bowl. Beat just until frothy. Dip each chicken breast in the egg white and then in the flour. Fry in 1/2 inch (1 cm) of hot oil until crisp and golden. Drain well. Cut the chicken into strips.

Combine the sugar, cornstarch, vinegar, lemon rind, lemon juice and chicken broth in a large saucepan. Boil until thick. Stir in the red and green pepper, carrot and green onions. Cook for 1 minute.

Arrange the chicken strips in a 9-by-13 inch (4 L) baking dish. Set the fruit around the edges. Pour the vegetables and sauce over the chicken. Cook in the oven until heated through, about 5 minutes.

This dish can be prepared ahead of time and reheated in the oven for 30 minutes.

Sticky Garlic Chicken

Serve Sticky Garlic Chicken out of a pretty bowl and have your guests eat the chicken with their fingers. Pick up each garlic clove, squeeze the skin and let the middle pop into your mouth.

PREPARATION TIME: 15 minutes
COOKING TIME: 15 minutes
YIELD: 4 servings

3 lb	chicken, cut into bite-size pieces	1.5 kg
2 Tbsp	peanut oil	25 mL
20 cloves	garlic, unpeeled	20 cloves
1/2	lemon	1/2
1/2 tsp	salt	2 mL
1/2 tsp	pepper	2 mL
2 Tbsp	brandy	25 mL

Sauté the chicken in the oil in a large frying pan for 5 minutes. Add the garlic. Squeeze the lemon over the chicken and sprinkle with the salt and pepper. Cover and cook for about 10 minutes until the skin of the garlic is transparent and chicken is cooked through. Pour in the brandy and flame with a match.

Serve with stir-fried vegetables or a green salad.

Chicken and Broccoli Stir Fry

Beautiful in appearance and sensational in taste, this dish is a fine addition to your collection of wok recipes.

PREPARATION TIME: 30 minutes
STANDING TIME: 15 minutes
COOKING TIME: 10 minutes
YIELD: 2 servings

1 whole	chicken breast, skinned, boned and cut into 1-inch (2.5 cm) cubes	1 whole
2-3 cloves	garlic, minced	2-3 cloves
3 Tbsp	oil	45 mL
2 Tbsp	soy sauce	25 mL
1/2 tsp	salt	2 mL
1/4 tsp	pepper	1 mL
2 tsp	cornstarch	10 mL
4	green onions, cut into 1/2-inch (12 mm) lengths	4
8-10	broccoli florets	8-10
1/4 tsp	sugar	1 mL
1/4 cup	cold water	50 mL
1/4 cup	slivered almonds	50 mL

Combine the cubed chicken, garlic, 1 tablespoon (15 mL) of oil, 1 tablespoon (15 mL) of soy sauce, salt, pepper and cornstarch. Let stand for 15 minutes.

Heat the remaining oil in a wok or frying pan. Sauté the onions and the broccoli for 2 to 3 minutes. Remove from the pan to a warm dish. Toss in the marinated chicken and cook, stirring, for 3 minutes.

Combine the remaining soy sauce, cornstarch, sugar and water. Add to the chicken along with the reserved vegetables. Cook for 3 minutes over low heat. Sprinkle with the slivered almonds and serve immediately.

This dish is best served over steamed white rice.

Barbecued Chicken

Because the chicken is broiled before the sauce is added, it does not get soggy as oven-barbecued chicken is wont to do.

PREPARATION TIME: 10 minutes
COOKING TIME: 40-50 minutes
YIELD: 4 servings

3 lb	chicken, cut into eight pieces	1.5 kg
1 tsp	garlic powder	5 mL
1 tsp	salt	5 mL
1 bottle (10-oz)	chili sauce	1 bottle (284 mL)
2 Tbsp	white wine vinegar	25 mL
2 Tbsp	brown sugar	25 mL
2 Tbsp	dry mustard	25 mL
2 Tbsp	Worcestershire sauce	25 mL
1/2 cup	water	125 mL
1 large	onion, chopped	1 large
1/2 cup	chopped celery	125 mL
1/2 cup	chopped green pepper	125 mL
1/2 cup	chopped mushrooms	125 mL

Preheat the oven to broil.

Sprinkle the chicken with the garlic powder and salt. Broil for 10 minutes on each side.

Meanwhile, combine the chili sauce, vinegar, brown sugar, mustard, Worcestershire sauce and water and simmer for 10 minutes. Add the chopped vegetables.

Set the oven temperature to 375°F (190°C). Pour the sauce over the chicken and bake for 40 to 50 minutes, basting regularly.

Serve over steamed white rice.

Fillets à l'Orange

This elegant and very easy entrée has a delicious tang that will have your guests asking for seconds.

PREPARATION TIME: 15 minutes
COOKING TIME: 20-30 minutes
YIELD: 4 servings

2 lb	sole or turbot fillets	1 kg
1/4 cup	sliced green onions	50 mL
2 Tbsp	butter	25 mL
3 Tbsp	flour	45 mL
1 Tbsp	sugar	15 mL
1/2 tsp	salt	2 mL
dash	freshly ground pepper	dash
1/2 cup	orange juice	125 mL
	juice of 1 lemon	
1/4 cup	coarsely chopped parsley	50 mL
1	orange, thinly sliced	1

Preheat the oven to 350°F (180°C).

Arrange the fillets in a greased 9-by-13 inch (4 L) pan. Sprinkle with the green onions.

Melt the butter and whisk it together with the flour, sugar, salt, pepper and orange and lemon juice. Drizzle over the fillets. Bake for 20 to 30 minutes, basting once after 5 minutes.

Sprinkle with parsley and garnish with the orange slices.

Greek Fish

The wonderful aroma of this dish as it cooks will remind travellers of pleasant days spent in the Greek isles.

PREPARATION TIME: **10 minutes**
COOKING TIME: **30 minutes**
YIELD: **4 servings**

2 medium	onions, chopped	2 medium
1 clove	garlic, minced	1 clove
2 Tbsp	chopped fresh parsley	25 mL
2 Tbsp	vegetable oil	25 mL
2	tomatoes, chopped	2
1 tsp	oregano	5 mL
1	bay leaf	1
	salt and freshly ground pepper to taste	
1/4 cup	white wine	50 mL
2 tsp	lemon juice	10 mL
1 lb	white fish fillets (cod, halibut or turbot)	500 g
	tomato and lemon slices as garnish	

Preheat the oven to 350°F (180°C).

Sauté the onions, garlic and parsley in the oil for 2 minutes. Add the tomatoes, oregano, bay leaf, salt and pepper. Sauté for 2 more minutes. Add the wine and lemon juice. Stir to mix well.

Put one-half of the vegetable mixture in a greased 10-by-6 inch (3 L) baking dish. Place the fish on top. Cover with the remaining vegetable mixture. Top with the tomato and lemon slices. Bake for 30 minutes.

Serve with white rice and a Greek salad.

Haddock in Hazelnut Sauce

Your local health food store will probably stock the hazelnuts called for in this recipe. It's worth the trip!

PREPARATION TIME: **10** minutes
COOKING TIME: **30** minutes
YIELD: **6** servings

2 lb	haddock fillets, skinned	1 kg
1 Tbsp	lemon juice	15 mL
	salt and freshly ground pepper to taste	
4 oz	ground hazelnuts (filberts)	125 g
1/4 cup	grated Cheddar cheese	50 mL
1/2 cup	milk	125 mL
pinch	nutmeg	pinch
1 Tbsp	sherry	15 mL
1/4 cup	fresh bread crumbs	50 mL
2 Tbsp	butter	25 mL

Preheat the oven to 400°F (200°C).

Cut the fish into slices. Brush with the lemon juice and sprinkle with salt and pepper. Place the fish in a greased baking dish.

Combine half the hazelnuts with the cheese, milk, nutmeg and sherry and pour over the fish. Mix the bread crumbs and the remaining hazelnuts and sprinkle on top of the fish. Dot with butter and bake for 30 minutes.

Halibut Thermidor

Use this dish for a buffet brunch or serve it for dinner over noodles. Halibut is a tasty substitute for shellfish.

PREPARATION TIME: 20 minutes
COOKING TIME: 30 minutes
YIELD: 6-8 servings

3 lb	halibut	1.35 kg
1/4 cup	butter	50 mL
1 small	onion, grated	1 small
8 oz	mushrooms, sliced	250 g
1 pt	10% cream	500 mL
1/4 cup	flour	50 mL
1 tsp	dry mustard	5 mL
1 1/2 tsp	salt	7.5 mL
dash	pepper	dash
2	egg yolks, lightly beaten	2
1 cup	process cheese spread	250 mL
1/4 cup	sherry	50 mL
1 Tbsp	lemon juice	15 mL

Steam the halibut. (This should take about 20 minutes.) Cool and break into chunks.

Melt the butter in a large saucepan and add the onion and mushrooms. Sauté until soft. Add the cream and flour, stirring constantly until thick. Add the mustard, salt and pepper. Mix the yolks and cheese into the hot mixture until the cheese melts. Add the sherry and lemon juice. Carefully spoon in the halibut pieces. Heat thoroughly.

This dish can be made ahead of time and reheated. It also freezes well.

Baked Stuffed Salmon

Our salmon makes an impressive main course for those special-occasion dinner parties.

PREPARATION TIME: **30 minutes**
COOKING TIME: **10 minutes for each inch (2.5 cm) of stuffed
thickness**
YIELD: **6 servings**

1/4 cup	butter	50 mL
1/2 cup	diced celery	125 mL
1/2 cup	diced onion	125 mL
4 cups	soft bread crumbs	1 L
2 cups	diced cucumber	500 mL
1 tsp	celery seed	5 mL
1 tsp	salt	5 mL
1/2 tsp	pepper	2 mL
4 lb	salmon, boned if desired	2 kg
	lemon wedges as garnish	

Preheat the oven to 450°F (230°C).

Melt the butter in a frying pan and sauté the celery and onion until soft but not brown. In a large bowl combine the remaining ingredients except for the salmon. Add the celery and onion mixture and combine thoroughly. Stuff the salmon loosely. Place skewers through the opening and lace with string. Place salmon on a greased baking dish. Measure the fish at its thickest point and bake for 10 minutes per inch (2.5 cm).

Slice and serve immediately with lemon wedges.

English Sole Provençale

Serve this tasty fish with rice to enjoy all of its savoury sauce.

PREPARATION TIME: 15 minutes
COOKING TIME: 15 minutes
YIELD: 4 servings

4 small	sole or haddock fillets	4 small
1 tsp	salt	5 mL
	freshly ground pepper	
	juice of 1 lemon	
1/4 cup	flour	50 mL
2 tsp	olive oil	10 mL
3 Tbsp	butter	45 mL
2	green onions, finely chopped	2
2 cloves	garlic, minced	2 cloves
2 large	tomatoes, chopped	2 large

Season the fish with the salt and pepper. Sprinkle with lemon juice. Dip lightly in the flour. Heat the oil and fry the fish until golden on both sides.

In another pan, melt the butter and sauté the onions and garlic for 2 minutes.

Add the tomatoes and cook for 5 minutes. Pour over the fish.

Serve immediately.

Sole with White Wine Sauce

The richness of the white wine sauce in this recipe is tempered by the subtle flavour of lemon. It complements the sole perfectly.

PREPARATION TIME: **10 minutes**
COOKING TIME: **20 minutes**
YIELD: **2 servings**

1/4 cup	butter	50 mL
2 Tbsp	chopped green onions	25 mL
3/4 cup	sliced mushrooms	175 mL
12 oz	sole fillets, fresh or frozen	375 g
1/2 cup	dry white wine	125 mL
2 Tbsp	flour	25 mL
1 tsp	lemon juice	5 mL
2 Tbsp	10% cream	25 mL
	parsley as garnish	

Melt half the butter in a large frying pan over medium heat. Arrange the onions and mushrooms evenly over the bottom of the pan. Place the fish fillets on top of the vegetables. Pour the wine over the fish. Bring to a boil then reduce the heat to medium-low. Cover and cook 10 to 12 minutes, until the fish flakes easily with a fork. Remove from heat.

Pour the cooking liquid into a measuring cup. Add water, if necessary, to make 3/4 cup (175 mL). In a small saucepan, melt the remaining butter over medium heat. Gradually add the flour, stirring constantly. Continue to cook until the mixture bubbles. Gradually stir in the lemon juice and fish liquid, stirring vigorously until thoroughly blended. Stir in the cream and heat until the mixture is smooth and heated through.

Pour the sauce over the fish and serve hot, garnished with parsley.

Curried Shrimp

It *is* possible to make a curry dish without using a cream sauce base and we prove it here without a doubt.

PREPARATION TIME: 10 minutes
COOKING TIME: 25 minutes
YIELD: 2 servings

1/4 cup	butter or margarine	50 mL
1 large	onion, finely chopped	1 large
3 Tbsp	flour	45 mL
1 cup	applesauce	250 mL
1 can	condensed beef bouillon	1 can
(10-oz)		(284 mL)
1 1/2 tsp	curry powder	7 mL
1/4 tsp	ground ginger	1 mL
1/4 tsp	salt	1 mL
dash	cayenne pepper	dash
2 Tbsp	lemon juice	25 mL
1 pkg	frozen shrimp, thawed	1 pkg
(10-oz) *or*		(283 g) *or*
1 1/2 cups	fresh shrimp	375 g

Melt the butter or margarine in a large frying pan. Add the onion and cook until tender, about 10 minutes.

Stir in the flour, applesauce, bouillon, curry powder, ginger, salt, cayenne and lemon juice. Blend well. Add the shrimp and simmer uncovered for about 10 minutes, until the shrimp are tender and the sauce has thickened.

Serve on a bed of rice with shredded coconut and mango chutney.

Note: If doubling the recipe, double only the quantity of shrimp.

Savoury Broiled Shrimp

Neptune himself would be honoured to be served this dish—one fit for a king.

PREPARATION TIME: 45 minutes
COOKING TIME: 15 minutes
YIELD: 4 servings

30	jumbo shrimp	30
5 Tbsp	butter	75 mL
2/3 cup	chopped onion	150 mL
2/3 cup	chopped celery	150 mL
1/2 tsp	minced garlic	2 mL
1/2 cup	chopped mushrooms	125 mL
	salt and freshy ground pepper to taste	
3/4 cup + 1 Tbsp	soft bread crumbs	175 mL + 15 mL
2 Tbsp	chopped parsley	25 mL
1	egg, lightly beaten	1

Preheat the oven to broil.

Peel and devein the shrimp. Set aside 20 to 24 shrimp. Coarsely chop the remaining shrimp.

Heat 2 tablespoons (25 mL) of butter in a saucepan. Add the onion, celery and garlic. Cook until wilted. Stir in the mushrooms, salt and pepper and cook for 3 minutes. Remove from the heat. Add the chopped shrimp, 3/4 cup (175 mL) bread crumbs, parsley and egg.

Split the reserved shrimp down the back but not all the way through. Open carefully, split side up, and spoon equal portions of stuffing on top of each shrimp.

Grease a metal or enamel baking dish large enough to hold all the shrimp in one layer. Arrange the shrimp in the dish. Sprinkle with the remaining bread crumbs and dot with the rest of the butter. Place the dish on the stove top over medium heat until the butter melts and the juice around the shrimp boils. Place the dish under the broiler for 5 minutes or until the shrimp are heated through and nicely browned.

Lamb Cupcakes

In both taste and shape, you will find our recipe a welcome change from traditional meat loaf.

PREPARATION TIME: **5 minutes**
COOKING TIME: **20-25 minutes**
YIELD: **12 muffins (4 servings)**

1 lb	ground lamb	500 g
8 oz	lean ground beef	250 g
2 cups	soft bread crumbs	500 mL
1 can	condensed onion soup	1 can
(10 1/2-oz)		(298 mL)
1/4 tsp	oregano	1 mL
	mint leaves as garnish	

Preheat the oven to 400°F (200°C).

Combine the ground meats, bread crumbs, soup and oregano. Spoon the mixture into 12 ungreased 2 1/2-inch (6 cm) muffin cups, pressing in lightly. Bake about 20 to 25 minutes, or until well browned. Garnish with the fresh mint.

Serve with mint jelly or tomato chutney.

Barbecue or Skillet Kebabs

A cross between a hamburger and a hot dog, this recipe provides a novel alternative to both of these barbecue standbys.

PREPARATION TIME: 10 minutes
COOKING TIME: 15 minutes
YIELD: 4 servings

1 lb	lean ground lamb or ground chicken	500 g
1 small	onion, minced	1 small
1 1/2 tsp	yogurt	7 mL
1 tsp	curry powder	5 mL
1/4 tsp	salt	1 mL
1 tsp	lemon juice	5 mL

Mix all the ingredients together thoroughly. Divide into 8 portions. Pat each portion around a skewer in a long cigar shape.

Cook over hot barbecue coals until brown all over. The kebabs can also be cooked in a frying pan with a shallow amount of very hot oil.

Veal à la Suisse

The combination of tarragon and Swiss cheese in the sauce produces an unusual and delicious taste sensation.

PREPARATION TIME: 15 minutes
COOKING TIME: 30 minutes
YIELD: 2-3 servings

1/4 cup	butter	50 mL
1 lb	veal scaloppine	500 g
	salt and pepper to taste	
1/4 tsp	tarragon	1 mL
1 small	onion, thinly sliced	1 small
8 oz	Swiss cheese, grated	250 g
1/4 cup	cracker crumbs	50 mL
1/2 cup	dry white wine	125 mL
1/2 can	undiluted consommé	1/2 can
(10-oz)		(284 mL)

Preheat the oven to 350°F (180°C).

Melt 2 tablespoons (25 mL) of the butter in a frying pan. Lightly brown the veal on both sides. Lay in a shallow buttered casserole dish. Sprinkle with salt, pepper and tarragon. Top the veal with the onion slices. Cover with the cheese and then the cracker crumbs. Dot with the remaining butter. Combine the wine and the consommé. Pour over the veal. Cover. Bake for 30 minutes, basting occasionally.

Serve with noodles or rice.

Veal and Prosciutto in Marsala

The beautiful colours and attractive presentation of this dish make a centrepiece for an elegant dinner.

PREPARATION TIME: 15 minutes
COOKING TIME: 15 minutes
YIELD: 4 servings

8 slices	veal scaloppine	8 slices
	salt and pepper	
2 Tbsp	flour	25 mL
3 Tbsp	olive oil	45 mL
6 Tbsp	butter	90 mL
1/2 cup	Marsala	125 mL
1 pkg	spinach, cooked	1 pkg
(10-oz)		(283 g)
4 slices	prosciutto ham	4 slices
2	eggs, hard-boiled and sliced	2
2 Tbsp	chopped fresh parsley	25 mL

Sprinkle the veal with salt and pepper; dredge lightly on both sides with flour. Heat the oil in a large frying pan. Cook the veal quickly in the hot oil until golden brown on both sides. Melt the butter in another frying pan. Transfer the veal to the second frying pan. Sprinkle with the Marsala. Cover and cook for 4 minutes. Uncover and cook 2 minutes until the sauce is slightly thickened.

Arrange equal portions of hot cooked spinach on 4 plates. Cover the spinach with 2 slices of veal. Top with a slice of prosciutto. Spoon the Marsala sauce over the meat. Arrange the egg slices on top. Sprinkle with parsley.

Veal Scaloppine with Mushrooms

Veal is always an impressive entrée; the beauty of this recipe is that it can be prepared ahead of time.

PREPARATION TIME: 15 minutes
COOKING TIME: 20 minutes
YIELD: 4-6 servings

1/2 cup	flour	125 mL
1 tsp	salt	5 mL
1/4 tsp	pepper	1 mL
1 1/2 lb	veal scaloppine	750 g
4-6 Tbsp	butter	50-90 mL
2 Tbsp	oil	25 mL
1 clove	garlic, halved	1 clove
8 oz	mushrooms, thinly sliced	250 g
2 Tbsp	lemon juice	25 mL
1/2 cup	dry white wine	125 mL
2/3 cup	chicken broth	150 mL
2 Tbsp	chopped fresh parsley	25 mL

Combine the flour with the salt and pepper in a shallow bowl. Coat the veal with the seasoned flour, shaking off the excess. Heat half of the butter and oil in a large frying pan; add the garlic. Brown the veal, 2 or 3 pieces at a time, for 2 to 3 minutes per side. Remove to a baking or serving dish and keep warm. Continue cooking the veal, adding the remaining butter and oil as necessary. Discard garlic.

If the frying pan is dry, add 1 tablespoon (15 mL) butter. Sauté the mushrooms until limp. Spread mushrooms over the veal. Stir the lemon juice, wine and broth into the frying pan. Cook for 1 minute over low heat, scraping up the brown bits. Pour the sauce over the veal. Sprinkle with parsley. Serve hot.

The recipe may be prepared up to the point of pouring the sauce over the veal, then cooled, covered and refrigerated. When ready to serve, bake for 30 minutes at 325°F (160°C).

Veal and Potato Pie

Hot and hearty, this simple family dish could well become a regular in your household.

PREPARATION TIME: 20 minutes
COOKING TIME: 30 minutes
YIELD: 4 servings

3-4 medium	potatoes	3-4 medium
3 Tbsp	butter	45 mL
1 large	onion, chopped	1 large
1 clove	garlic, chopped	1 clove
1 1/2 lb	ground veal or ground lean beef	700 g
1 can (5 1/2-oz)	tomato paste	1 can (156 mL)
2 tsp	Worcestershire sauce	10 mL
1	bay leaf	1
1 tsp	thyme	5 mL
2-3 drops	Tabasco sauce	2-3 drops
	salt and pepper to taste	
1/2 cup	milk, heated slightly	125 mL
1 1/2 Tbsp	dried parsley	20 mL
dash	nutmeg	dash
1/4 cup	grated Parmesan cheese	50 mL

Peel and dice the potatoes. Boil until cooked through.

Melt 1 tablespoon (15 mL) butter in a separate saucepan. Add the onion and garlic and cook until limp. Add the meat, tomato paste, Worcestershire sauce, bay leaf, thyme, Tabasco, salt and pepper. Stir to combine. Cover and simmer for 20 minutes, stirring occasionally.

Preheat the oven to broil.

Drain and mash the potatoes with the remaining butter and the milk. Whip in the parsley and nutmeg.

Discard the bay leaf from the meat mixture and drain off any excess liquid.

Spoon into a flameproof dish or casserole. Smooth the potatoes over the meat and sprinkle with the cheese. Broil for 3 minutes, or until the top has browned.

Serve with a fresh salad and your favourite vegetable.

Savoury Sautéed Veal Chops

Do not be concerned about the large number of garlic cloves called for in this recipe. The flavour is subtle enough so as not to overwhelm the delicate taste of the veal.

PREPARATION TIME: 15 minutes
COOKING TIME: 30 minutes
YIELD: 4 servings

4	loin veal chops	4
	salt and freshly ground	
	black pepper	
1/4 cup	butter	50 mL
20 cloves	garlic, peeled	20 cloves
2	bay leaves	2
1/2 tsp	thyme	2 mL
2 Tbsp	red wine vinegar	25 mL
3/4 cup	chicken broth	175 mL

Sprinkle both sides of the chops with salt and pepper. Melt the butter in a large frying pan and add the chops. Over high heat brown chops for 2 minutes on each side, watching carefully that they do not burn. Reduce the heat to medium and add the garlic, bay leaves and thyme. Cook for 3 minutes.

Pour the vinegar around the chops and increase the heat, stirring up the brown bits on the bottom of the pan. Add the broth and bring to a boil. Reduce the heat so liquid simmers, cover and cook for 20 minutes. Spoon the sauce over the chops.

Serve with wild rice and steamed carrots or broccoli.

Good and Spicy Meatballs

These flavourful nuggets work equally well as a main course or an appetizer.

PREPARATION TIME: **15 minutes**
COOKING TIME: **20 minutes**
YIELD: **4 main course or 8 appetizer servings**

Meatballs

1/2 cup	cornflake crumbs	125 mL
1 lb	ground beef	500 g
2 Tbsp	ketchup	25 mL
2/3 cup	non-fat milk powder	150 mL
1 tsp	salt	5 mL
pinch	pepper	pinch
1	egg	1
1/4 cup	grated onion	50 mL
1/4 cup	water	50 mL

Sauce

1/4 cup	ketchup	50 mL
1 can	tomato sauce	1 can
(7 1/2-oz)		(213 mL)
2 Tbsp	brown sugar	25 mL
pinch	pepper	pinch
1 Tbsp	Worcestershire sauce	15 mL
1/4 cup	water	50 mL
1 Tbsp	vinegar	15 mL

Preheat the oven to 400°F (200°C).

Meatballs: Combine the meatball ingredients. Shape into 1-inch (2.5 cm) meatballs and place in a single layer in a foil-lined shallow baking dish. Bake for 12 minutes or until browned.

Sauce: While the meatballs are cooking, combine the sauce ingredients in a 3-quart (3 L) saucepan. Simmer over moderate heat about 15 minutes, stirring frequently. Add the meatballs and keep warm until serving time.

Serve over rice or noodles.

Paprika Pepper Steak

The rich, red paprika colour of this hearty dish is enhanced by fluffy white rice or broad egg noodles.

PREPARATION TIME: 15 minutes
COOKING TIME: 30 minutes
YIELD: 4-6 servings

1 1/2 lb	sirloin steak, cut across the grain into thin strips	750 g
1 Tbsp	paprika	15 mL
1/2 tsp	cayenne pepper	2 mL
1 medium	onion	1 medium
2	green peppers	2
4 oz	mushrooms	125 g
2 cloves	garlic, crushed	2 cloves
2 Tbsp	butter	25 mL
2 large	tomatoes, chopped	2 large
1/2 cup	beef broth	125 mL
1/2 cup	red wine	125 mL
2 Tbsp	soy sauce	25 mL
1/4 cup	water	50 mL
2 Tbsp	cornstarch	25 mL

Sprinkle the steak with paprika and cayenne pepper, and stir to coat. Slice the onion, green peppers and mushrooms, and reserve. Sauté the steak and garlic in the butter until the meat is brown. Add the reserved vegetables and cook until they are tender-crisp. Add the tomatoes, broth, wine and soy sauce. Cover and simmer for 15 minutes.

Combine the water and cornstarch. Add to the meat mixture and boil until thickened (about 1 minute).

Serve over rice or egg noodles.

Oriental Fantasia

Add rice or noodles to this colourful medley of beef and vegetables to make a complete meal.

PREPARATION TIME: **20** minutes
COOKING TIME: **10** minutes
YIELD: **4** servings

2 Tbsp	dry sherry	25 mL
1/2 tsp	sugar	2 mL
1 tsp	cornstarch	5 mL
3 Tbsp	soy sauce	45 mL
1 Tbsp	sesame oil	15 mL
	pepper to taste	
1 lb	flank steak or inside round	500 g
1/2	green pepper	1/2
1/2	red pepper	1/2
3	scallions	3
1/4 cup	celery	50 mL
4 oz	mushrooms	125 g
4 oz	snow peas	125 g
2-3 Tbsp	oil	25-45 mL
2 cloves	garlic, chopped	2 cloves
2 slices	ginger root	2 slices
1/4 cup	slivered almonds	50 mL

Combine the sherry, sugar, cornstarch, soy sauce, sesame oil and pepper in a large bowl. Slice the beef into 1/4-inch (5 mm) slices, against the grain. Add the beef to the marinade and mix to coat.

While the beef is marinating, slice the green and red pepper into slivers. Slice the scallions on a diagonal into 1/2-inch (1.25 cm) pieces. Cut the celery into 1/4-inch (5 mm) slices. Thinly slice the mushrooms.

Put 1 tablespoon (15 mL) of oil in a heated wok or frying pan. Heat the oil to the smoking point. Stir-fry the peppers, scallions, celery, mushrooms and snow peas for 2 to 3 minutes. Do not overcook. Remove the vegetables from the wok.

Add 1 to 2 teaspoons (5 to 10 mL) oil to the wok. Add the garlic and ginger and stir-fry briefly. Do not allow the garlic to brown.

Add 1 tablespoon (15 mL) oil to the wok. Add the beef. Stir-fry quickly for 3 to 4 minutes, until just a few spots of pink remain. Add the vegetables and the almonds to the wok. Stir-fry the entire mixture for approximately 2 minutes.

Serve with rice or Chinese noodles.

Pork Chops with Madeira Sauce

The simplicity of this recipe makes it ideal to prepare after a hectic day.

PREPARATION TIME: 5 minutes
COOKING TIME: 25 minutes
YIELD: 4 servings

4	loin pork chops	4
	freshly ground pepper	
1 tsp	vegetable oil	5 mL
2-3 Tbsp	Madeira	25-45 mL
1/2 cup	sour cream	125 mL

Preheat the oven to 225°F (110°C).

Sprinkle the pork chops with pepper. Heat the oil in a heavy frying pan. Cook the chops slowly on one side, about 10 minutes. Turn and continue cooking until done, about 10 more minutes. Remove the chops from the pan and keep warm in the oven.

Deglaze the pan with Madeira. Add the sour cream and mix with a wooden spoon. Return the chops to the pan and stir until completely covered with the sauce.

Serve immediately with a brightly coloured vegetable.

Pork Chops with Apple-Mustard Sauce

Even those not partial to pork will become pork chop lovers after sampling this dish.

PREPARATION TIME: **10 minutes**
COOKING TIME: **30 minutes**
YIELD: **4 servings**

4	loin pork chops	4
2 Tbsp	butter	25 mL
1 cup	apple juice	250 mL
1 medium	onion, sliced	1 medium
1 clove	garlic, minced	1 clove
1/2 tsp	thyme	2 mL
1 Tbsp	flour	15 mL
4 tsp	Dijon mustard	20 mL
1 medium	apple, cored and sliced	1 medium
	parsley as garnish	

Trim the pork chops and flatten slightly with a cleaver. Melt the butter in a large frying pan. Add the pork chops and brown on both sides. Add the apple juice, onion, garlic and thyme. Cover and cook for 10 to 12 minutes.

Remove the chops and keep warm.

Bring the liquid to a boil and add the flour and mustard. Stir the mixture until well blended, scraping up the brown bits from the bottom of the pan. Add the apple slices and heat briefly. Pour the sauce over the chops. Sprinkle with parsley and serve immediately.

EGG, CHEESE & BRUNCH DISHES

Egg Puff Pancake

The versatility of this simple dish is limited only by the boundaries of your imagination. The following is the recipe for the basic version.

PREPARATION TIME: **5 minutes**
COOKING TIME: **20 minutes**
YIELD: **2 servings**

1/2 cup	flour	125 mL
1/2 cup	milk	125 mL
2	eggs, lightly beaten	2
pinch	nutmeg	pinch
1/4 cup	unsalted butter	50 mL

Preheat the oven to 425°F (220°C).

Combine the flour, milk, eggs and nutmeg. Beat lightly, leaving the batter slightly lumpy.

Melt the butter in a large ovenproof frying pan. When the butter is bubbling, pour the batter into the frying pan—do not mix—and immediately place in the oven. Bake for 20 minutes or until golden brown.

For a brunch or breakfast dish, serve with maple syrup, jam, cinnamon sugar or applesauce. As a dessert, this can be served with ice cream or whipped cream.

Sweet Version: Try it with 1 chopped apple, 2 teaspoons (10 mL) sugar and 1 tablespoon (15 mL) Grand Marnier added to the batter. Increase the cooking time by 5 minutes.

Savoury Version: Omit the nutmeg and use salted butter. Add salt, pepper and your choice of herbs and spices for seasoning.

Eggs Baked in Tomatoes

Although these eggs require careful preparation, the lovely presentation and delicious taste justify the effort.

PREPARATION TIME: **15 minutes**
COOKING TIME: **30-40 minutes**
YIELD: **6 servings**

6 medium	tomatoes, ripe but very firm	6 medium
2 tsp	salt	10 mL
2 Tbsp	butter	25 mL
1 tsp	sugar	5 mL
6	eggs	6
1/2 tsp	basil	2 mL
	salt and pepper to taste	
1/4 cup	grated Swiss cheese	50 mL

Preheat the oven to 350°F (180°C).

Cut a thin slice off the top of each tomato. Scoop out as much pulp as possible, taking care not to break the skin. Leave the ribs to support the shape of the tomato. Salt the insides and turn upside down for 15 minutes so the excess juices drain.

Butter a baking dish with 1 tablespoon (15 mL) butter. Place the tomatoes in the dish. Sprinkle the sugar in the shells and put 1/4 teaspoon (1 mL) butter in each shell. Bake for 10 minutes.

Break an egg inside each tomato. Sprinkle with basil, salt and pepper. Divide the cheese equally and sprinkle over the eggs. Bake for 30 to 40 minutes, until the eggs are set.

Eggs for Two

Our classy scrambled eggs will make your brunch or late-night supper something special.

PREPARATION TIME: 5 minutes
COOKING TIME: 10 minutes
YIELD: 2 servings

5	eggs	5
	salt and pepper to taste	
1 Tbsp	minced fresh herbs (chives, parsley, chervil)	15 mL
1 clove	garlic, peeled	1 clove
2 Tbsp	unsalted butter	25 mL
2 Tbsp	sour cream, room temperature	25 mL
2	English muffins, split and toasted	2
1 Tbsp	caviar (optional)	15 mL

Break the eggs into a bowl. Add the salt and pepper and the herbs. Spear the garlic clove on a fork and gently beat the eggs with it.

Melt butter in the top of a double-boiler over hot water. Add the eggs and cook, stirring continuously, until they are the consistency of custard, about 10 minutes. Remove from the heat and stir in the sour cream.

Serve on the toasted English muffins and sprinkle with the caviar if desired.

Note: Dried herbs are not suitable for this dish.

Eggs South Yemen

This attractive and colourful egg dish is appropriate for a light supper or breakfast for a weekend guest.

PREPARATION TIME: 10 minutes
COOKING TIME: 10 minutes
YIELD: 2 servings

2 Tbsp	butter	25 mL
1 small	onion, chopped	1 small
1 clove	garlic, minced	1 clove
2 large	tomatoes, thickly sliced	2 large
	salt and pepper to taste	
4	eggs	4
4 slices	toast	4 slices
	chopped fresh parsley as garnish	

Melt the butter in a large frying pan. Sauté the onion and garlic in the butter until soft but not browned. Place the tomato slices on top of the onions. Sprinkle with salt and pepper. Cook the tomatoes for 2 minutes, turn over and cook for another 2 minutes. Break the eggs on top of the tomatoes. Cover and cook for 4 minutes.

Serve on toast, garnished with parsley.

Cheese Puff

Easy to prepare, this mild-tasting Cheese Puff will be a hit at your next brunch.

PREPARATION TIME: **10 minutes**
COOKING TIME: **50 minutes**
YIELD: **6 servings**

12 oz	Monterey Jack cheese, grated	375 g
1 cup	biscuit mix	250 mL
1/2 cup	milk	125 mL
4	eggs	4
3 Tbsp	cottage cheese	45 mL
6 Tbsp	butter, cut into small pieces	90 mL
dash	freshly ground black pepper	dash

Preheat the oven to 350°F (180°C).

Combine all the ingredients in a large bowl and mix well.

Turn into a 2-quart (2 L) round baking dish.

Bake 50 minutes, until puffed and golden.

Double Cheese Casserole

Vegetarians will love this main-dish casserole, which rises like a soufflé and is a good source of protein.

PREPARATION TIME: 15 minutes
COOKING TIME: 45 minutes
YIELD: 4 servings

1/4 cup	butter	50 mL
6 Tbsp	flour	90 mL
2 dashes	cayenne pepper	2 dashes
3/4 tsp	dry mustard	3 mL
1/4 tsp	salt	1 mL
1/4 tsp	pepper	1 mL
6	eggs, separated	6
1 lb	large curd cottage cheese	500 g
1 pkg	frozen chopped broccoli,	1 pkg
(10-oz)	thawed	(283 g)
8 oz	Cheddar cheese, cubed	250 g

Preheat the oven to 350°F (180°C).

Melt butter and pour into a bowl. Stir in the flour, cayenne, dry mustard, salt and pepper.

Beat the egg yolks and add to the mixture. Stir in the cottage cheese and broccoli. Beat the egg whites until stiff peaks form. Fold gently into the mixture. Mix in the cubed cheese.

Pour into a greased 2-quart (2 L) casserole dish. Bake for 45 minutes.

This will make a nice breakfast or brunch dish when prepared without the broccoli.

Three-Pepper Pies

This recipe makes two incredible quiche-like pies. If you are cooking for a smaller group, try freezing the second pie to enjoy on another occasion.

PREPARATION TIME: 30 minutes
COOKING TIME: 30 minutes
YIELD: 16 servings

2 (9-in)	deep dish pie shells	2 (22 cm)
3 Tbsp	Dijon mustard	45 mL
1 1/2 cups	grated Emmenthal cheese	375 mL
3 Tbsp	butter	45 mL
3	onions, chopped	3
2 cloves	garlic, chopped	2 cloves
2	red peppers, diced	2
1	green pepper, diced	1
1	yellow pepper, diced	1
3 Tbsp	chopped parsley	45 mL
3	eggs	3
1 cup	35% cream	250 mL
1/2 tsp	salt	2 mL
1/4 tsp	freshly ground pepper	1 mL
dash	freshly ground nutmeg	dash
pinch	cayenne pepper	pinch

Preheat the oven to 375°F (190°C).

Brush the pie shells with the mustard and sprinkle each one with 1 1/2 tablespoons (20 mL) of cheese. Prick each one 4 or 5 times with a fork. Bake for 15 minutes.

Heat the butter in a large frying pan. Sauté the onions and garlic until tender. Add the peppers and continue cooking until all the vegetables are tender. Remove the pan from the heat and allow to cool slightly.

Distribute the vegetables in the 2 pie shells. Cover with the remaining cheese and sprinkle with the parsley. Beat the eggs, cream and spices, and divide the mixture between the 2 pies.

Bake for 30 minutes, or until the tops are golden brown. Set on a wire rack to cool slightly before cutting.

Serve with a green salad and white wine.

Super Simple Spinach Torte

For the health- or diet-conscious, this dish is a perfect substitute for quiche—it is neither as rich nor as high in cholesterol as the famous French pie.

PREPARATION TIME: **10 minutes**
COOKING TIME: **20-25 minutes**
YIELD: **2 servings**

1 pkg (10-oz)	frozen spinach	1 pkg (283 g)
or 1 bunch	fresh spinach	*or* 1 bunch
1	egg	1
2 Tbsp	melted butter or margarine	25 mL
3 Tbsp	grated Parmesan cheese	45 mL
1 cup	cottage cheese	250 mL
1-2	green onions, finely chopped	1-2
	salt and freshly ground pepper to taste	

Preheat the oven to 350°F (180°C).

Cook the spinach briefly. Drain, pressing out as much liquid as possible, then chop.

Beat the egg slightly and combine with the spinach and remaining ingredients. Pour the mixture into a buttered 8-inch (20 cm) pie plate.

Bake for 20 to 25 minutes, or until set. Let stand for 10 minutes before serving. The torte will set further during this time.

Serve with French bread and a tossed salad.

Salmon Soufflé

The secret of preparing a successful soufflé is to beat the egg whites until very stiff and to serve immediately.

PREPARATION TIME: 15 minutes
COOKING TIME: 35-40 minutes
YIELD: 4 servings

1 can	Sockeye salmon	1 can
(7 1/2-oz)		(202 g)
1/2 cup	butter, melted and cooled slightly	125 mL
1 large	onion, finely chopped	1 large
3/4 cup	sour cream	175 mL
3	eggs, separated	3
3/4 cup	bread crumbs	175 mL
1/2 tsp	garlic powder	2 mL
1 Tbsp	finely chopped fresh dill	15 mL
1 Tbsp	finely chopped fresh parsley	15 mL
	salt and pepper to taste	
pinch	cream of tartar	pinch
1/4 cup	grated Parmesan or Romano cheese	50 mL

Preheat the oven to 375°F (190°C).

Combine the salmon, butter, onion, sour cream, egg yolks, 1/2 cup (125 mL) bread crumbs, garlic, dill, parsley, salt and pepper in the container of a blender. Purée until smooth. Set aside.

Beat the egg whites and cream of tartar until they stand in stiff peaks. Gently fold into the salmon mixture until combined. Spoon into a buttered soufflé dish.

Combine the remaining bread crumbs with the cheese and sprinkle on top. Bake for 35 to 40 minutes, or until golden brown. Serve immediately.

Super Salmon Pie

Because you will probably have all the ingredients required for this recipe on hand, it is perfect for last minute entertaining.

PREPARATION TIME: 15 minutes
COOKING TIME: 40 minutes
YIELD: 6 servings

Crust	1 cup	flour	250 mL
	1 Tbsp	sugar	15 mL
	1/2 tsp	salt	2 mL
	1/2 cup	grated Cheddar cheese	125 mL
	1/3 cup	oil	75 mL
	2 Tbsp	milk	25 mL

Filling	2 cans	salmon, drained	2 cans
	(7 1/2-oz)		(213 g)
	2	eggs, beaten	2
	3/4 cup	milk	175 mL
	1/4 tsp	salt	1 mL
	1/4 tsp	pepper	1 mL
	1 Tbsp	white vinegar or lemon juice	15 mL
		grated cheese as garnish	

Preheat the oven to 350°F (180°C).

Crust: Combine all the ingredients. Press into the bottom and sides of a 9-inch (22 cm) pie plate.

Filling: Combine the filling ingredients. Pour into the pie shell. Sprinkle with the additional grated cheese. Bake for 40 minutes.

Tuna Noodle Pie

We like the combination of the cheesy crust and noodle filling.

PREPARATION TIME: **20 minutes**
COOKING TIME: **35-40 minutes**
YIELD: **4 servings**

	1 cup	egg noodles	250 mL
Crust	1/4 cup	butter	50 mL
	3/4 cup	grated Cheddar cheese	175 mL
	3/4 cup	all-purpose flour	175 mL
	1/2 tsp	salt	2 mL
	1/4 tsp	dry mustard	1 mL
Filling	1 medium	onion, minced	1 medium
	2 Tbsp	butter	25 mL
	1 can	tuna, drained	1 can
	(6 1/2-oz)		(184 g)
	2	eggs, beaten	2
	1 cup	milk	250 mL
	1/4 tsp	pepper	1 mL
	1/4 cup	grated Cheddar cheese	50 mL

Preheat the oven to 350°F (180°C).

Cook the noodles according to package instructions. Drain.

Crust: Melt the butter and combine with the remaining crust ingredients in a medium-size bowl. Press the mixture into a greased 9-inch (1 L) pie plate.

Filling: Sauté the onions in the butter in a large frying pan set over medium-high heat, until transparent. Add the noodles and tuna. Mix well and pour into crust.

Combine the eggs, milk and pepper. Pour over the tuna mixture. Sprinkle with the grated Cheddar cheese. Bake for 35 to 40 minutes until the cheese is bubbling.

Note: Salmon may be substituted for the tuna.

Tofu French Toast

While this unusual French toast is a perfect breakfast or brunch dish, it also makes an interesting dessert when served with fruit.

PREPARATION TIME: 5 minutes
COOKING TIME: 5 minutes
YIELD: 4 servings

1 1/2 cups	tofu	375 mL
(3 cubes)		(3 cubes)
1 tsp	cinnamon	5 mL
1/4 cup	honey	50 mL
1/2 tsp	salt	2 mL
4 slices	bread	4 slices
2 Tbsp	butter or oil	25 mL

In a blender or food processor blend the tofu, cinnamon, honey and salt until smooth and creamy. Pour into a shallow bowl. Dip the bread in the batter and fry in the butter or oil in a frying pan until brown on both sides.

Serve as you would egg-batter French toast—with maple syrup, jam, butter, etc.

Apple Cheese Pancakes

At the cottage or on a lazy Sunday morning these pancakes will be a sure-fire hit with your brunch guests.

PREPARATION TIME: **10** minutes
SITTING TIME: **1** hour
COOKING TIME: **20** minutes
YIELD: **6** servings

1 cup	cottage cheese	250 mL
1 cup	applesauce	250 mL
1/4 cup	all-purpose flour	50 mL
1/2 cup	whole wheat flour	125 mL
1 Tbsp	honey	15 mL
1/4 tsp	lemon juice	1 mL
dash	cinnamon	dash
dash	nutmeg	dash
4	eggs, separated	4
	butter for frying	

Combine all the ingredients except the egg whites. Beat the egg whites until stiff and fold into the batter. Let the batter sit for 1 hour.

Heat the butter until sizzling, but not smoking, in a low-sided frying pan. Drop the batter by tablespoons into the pan. Flip the pancakes when small holes appear around the edges. Add more butter to the pan as required.

Serve with yogurt, fruit or maple syrup.

Variation: Add 1/4 cup (50 mL) of chopped nuts, sunflower seeds or raisins to the batter before folding in the egg whites.

PASTA & RICE

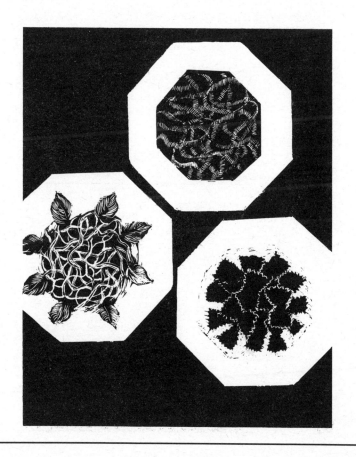

Green, Red and White Fettucine

Bearing the colours of the Italian flag, this pasta dish will brighten any table.

PREPARATION TIME: **10 minutes**
COOKING TIME: **10 minutes**
YIELD: **4 servings**

1 can (7-oz)	red Sockeye salmon	1 can (198 g)
2 Tbsp	lemon juice	25 mL
3 Tbsp	butter	45 mL
1	scallion, finely chopped	1
1/2 pt	18% cream	250 mL
1/4 cup	grated Parmesan cheese	50 mL
12 oz	spinach fettucine noodles	350 g
2 stalks	fresh dill, finely chopped (reserve 4 sprigs for garnish)	2 stalks
1 Tbsp	capers	15 mL
	freshly ground black pepper to taste	
	lemon slices as garnish	

Remove the skin and bones from the salmon and discard. Break salmon into small chunks. Toss with the lemon juice.

Melt the butter in a saucepan and add the scallion. Sauté over medium heat until tender. Stir in the cream and the Parmesan cheese.

Cook noodles in boiling salted water until 'al dente'. Drain and combine with the cream mixture. Remove from the heat and add the marinated salmon. Season with the dill, capers and black pepper.

Toss and serve immediately. Garnish each serving with a paper-thin lemon slice and a sprig of dill.

Serve with a piquant Caesar salad.

Linguine with Clam Sauce

Honey adds a nice touch to this unconventional clam sauce recipe.

PREPARATION TIME: 10 minutes
COOKING TIME: 45 minutes
YIELD: 4 servings

2 medium	onions, chopped	2 medium
1 clove	garlic, crushed	1 clove
2 Tbsp	olive oil	25 mL
1	bay leaf	1
1/4 tsp	basil	1 mL
1 tsp	salt	5 mL
pinch	freshly ground black pepper	pinch
2 tsp	honey	10 mL
1/4 cup	dry white wine	50 mL
1/4 cup	finely chopped parsley	50 mL
1 can	tomatoes	1 can
(13-oz)		(375 mL)
1 can	baby clams	1 can
(10 1/2-oz)		(284 mL)
1 lb	linguine	500 g
	grated Parmesan cheese	

Sauté the onions and the garlic in the olive oil. Add the remaining ingredients except the clams, linguine and cheese but include the clam liquor. Simmer uncovered for 40 minutes. Stir in the clams and heat for 5 more minutes.

Prepare the pasta according to the package instructions. Top with the clam sauce and sprinkle with the Parmesan cheese.

Lemon Clam Sauce for Pasta

The addition of lemon and the omission of white wine make this recipe a welcome addition to your clam sauce repertoire.

PREPARATION TIME: 10 minutes
COOKING TIME: 15 minutes
YIELD: 3-4 servings

1 Tbsp	butter	15 mL
1 large clove	garlic, minced	1 large clove
1 medium	onion, chopped	1 medium
1 can	clams, drained (save the	1 can
(10-oz)	liquid)	(284 mL)
1/2 tsp	crushed black peppercorns	2 mL
1 tsp	grated lemon rind	5 mL
2 tsp	chopped fresh basil	10 mL
1 Tbsp	cornstarch	15 mL
1 1/2 tsp	cold water	7 mL
1 cup	10% cream	250 mL
1 lb	linguine	500 g
	freshly grated Parmesan cheese	

Melt the butter in a frying pan over medium heat. Cook the garlic and onion until soft, not brown. Add the clam liquid, peppercorns, lemon rind and 1 teaspoon (5 mL) of basil. Cook a few minutes until the mixture is at a full simmer.

Mix the cornstarch and water. Add to the frying pan along with the clams. Bring almost to a boil. The mixture will be quite stiff. Add the cream. Keep sauce warm over low heat.

Cook the pasta according to the package instructions.

Drain the pasta well and toss with the clam sauce. Sprinkle with the remaining basil and freshly grated Parmesan cheese before serving.

Vermicelli and Clam Sauce

The combination of clams and cream make this a perfect light summer meal. All you need to add is a salad.

PREPARATION TIME: 10 minutes
COOKING TIME: 30 minutes
YIELD: 4-6 servings

2 cloves	garlic, minced	2 cloves
1 large	onion, chopped	1 large
2 Tbsp	vegetable oil	25 mL
2 cans (10-oz)	whole baby clams	2 cans (284 mL)
2 Tbsp	chopped fresh parsley	25 mL
1 tsp	rosemary	5 mL
1 tsp	thyme	5 mL
	salt and pepper to taste	
1 pt	18% cream	500 mL
12 oz	vermicelli, or egg noodles, cooked and drained	375 g

Sauté the garlic and onion in oil. Add the juice from the 2 cans of clams. Add the parsley, rosemary, thyme, salt and pepper. Simmer for 20 minutes.

Add the cream and clams and heat through.

Pour over the cooked vermicelli and stir.

Pasta with Shrimp and Pernod

This elegant dish has an unusual blend of flavours. It is delicious served with a Caesar salad or a simple green salad.

PREPARATION TIME: **20 minutes**
COOKING TIME: **30 minutes**
YIELD: **4 servings**

1 lb	linguine or spaghetti	450 g
1 clove	garlic, crushed	1 clove
3 Tbsp	butter	45 mL
1 lb	medium shrimp, peeled	500 g
1/2	sweet red pepper, sliced	1/2
1 cup	18% cream	250 mL
	grated rind of 1 lemon	
1/2 cup	fresh lemon juice	125 mL
1/2 cup	Pernod	125 mL
	grated Parmesan cheese as garnish	

Cook the pasta until 'al dente'. Sauté the garlic briefly in the butter. Add the shrimp and the red pepper and cook for a few minutes until the shrimp is pink. Lower the heat and add the cream and lemon rind. Simmer for 4 to 5 minutes. Stir in the lemon juice and Pernod. Add the drained pasta. Toss well. Raise the heat to medium and cook until the sauce thickens, stirring constantly.

Serve immediately with a generous sprinkling of grated Parmesan cheese.

Pebbly Pasta

This tasty recipe can be included in that marvelous genre of one-dish meals. For company, just add a fresh salad and garlic bread.

PREPARATION TIME: 25 minutes
COOKING TIME: 35 minutes
YIELD: 6 servings

2 Tbsp	oil	25 mL
1 clove	garlic, chopped	1 clove
1 1/2 lb	lean ground beef	750 g
2 medium	onions, chopped	2 medium
2	green onions, chopped	2
2	green peppers, chopped	2
5 stalks	celery, sliced	5 stalks
1 can	tomato paste	1 can
(5 1/2-oz)		(156 mL)
1 cup	water	250 mL
1/4 cup	soy sauce	50 mL
1 tsp	sugar	5 mL
8 oz	small shell pasta	250 g
	salt and pepper to taste	
	grated Parmesan cheese	
	(optional)	

Heat the oil in a heavy frying pan. Sauté the garlic and beef until the meat has almost lost its pink colour. Add the onions, peppers and celery and continue cooking for 10 minutes. Combine the tomato paste, water, soy sauce and sugar. Stir into the meat mixture. Simmer, uncovered, for 35 minutes.

Cook the pasta, drain and add to the meat mixture. Toss, add salt and pepper to taste and serve hot.

Grated Parmesan cheese may be sprinkled on top if desired.

Ravioli

Your guests will think you have been working in the kitchen all day to prepare this traditional Italian dish. The secret is in using wonton wrappers instead of pasta.

PREPARATION TIME: **25 minutes**
COOKING TIME: **10 minutes**
YIELD: **4-6 servings**

1 lb	ricotta cheese	500 g
1 extra large	egg	1 extra large
1/4 cup	grated Parmesan cheese	50 mL
2 Tbsp	chopped fresh parsley	25 mL
	salt and pepper to taste	
1 lb	wonton or egg roll wrappers*	500 g
1 can	spaghetti sauce	1 can
(26 1/4-oz)		(750 mL)
1 lb	Italian sausage	500 g
1 large	tomato, chopped	1 large

Combine the ricotta cheese, egg, Parmesan cheese, parsley, salt and pepper. Place a spoonful of filling on each wrapper. Wet the edge of the wrapper with a moistened finger. Fold into a triangle and seal firmly. Let the ravioli stand for 5 minutes. Place the ravioli in a large pot of boiling water. Boil for 10 minutes.

Empty the spaghetti sauce into a saucepan. Cut the sausage into thick slices and sauté until browned. Add sausage to the spaghetti sauce, reserving drippings. Sauté the tomato in the sausage drippings and add to the sauce.

Drain the ravioli; stir gently into the sauce. Serve immediately.

*Available fresh in the vegetable section of the supermarket or frozen in the deli section.

Linguine in Cream Sauce

This unusual pasta dish may be served as a side dish or entrée.

PREPARATION TIME: 30 minutes
COOKING TIME: 25 minutes
YIELD: 4 servings

2 cloves	garlic, crushed	2 cloves
1 Tbsp	butter	15 mL
8 oz	sweet Italian sausage, removed from casing and crumbled	250 g
2 Tbsp	chopped fresh basil	25 mL
1/4 cup	chopped fresh parsley	50 mL
10 medium	mushrooms, sliced	10 medium
1 tsp	flour	5 mL
1 cup	35% cream	250 mL
1/2 cup	freshly grated Parmesan cheese	125 mL
1 lb	linguine	500 g
	pepper to taste	

Sauté the garlic in butter for 1 to 2 minutes. Add the sausage and sauté 10 minutes. Add the basil, parsley and mushrooms and cook 3 minutes. Sprinkle the flour into the mixture, stir and cook for 2 minutes.

Add the cream and cheese and let it heat through, stirring constantly.

Cook the linguine, add to mixture and stir until mixed. Add pepper to taste.

Vegeroni

Both children and adults will enjoy this flavourful multi-coloured pasta. It can be served as a vegetarian main dish or as an accompaniment to a meat entrée.

PREPARATION TIME: **30 minutes**
COOKING TIME: **30 minutes**
YIELD: **6 servings**

2 Tbsp	butter	25 mL
1 clove	garlic, chopped	1 clove
1 medium	onion, chopped	1 medium
1 small	green pepper, chopped	1 small
4 oz	mushrooms, sliced	125 g
1 can	tomatoes	1 can
(14-oz)		(398 mL)
1/3 cup	tomato paste	75 mL
1/2 tsp	basil	2 mL
1/2 tsp	oregano	2 mL
1/4 tsp	tarragon	1 mL
1/4 tsp	cumin	1 mL
pinch	marjoram	pinch
	salt and pepper to taste	
1/4 tsp	soy sauce	1 mL
2 cups	vegeroni (multi-coloured macaroni)*	500 mL
8 oz	old Cheddar cheese, grated	250 g

Melt the butter in a large saucepan. Sauté the garlic, onion, pepper and mushrooms. Add the tomatoes and tomato paste. Mix well. Add the basil, oregano, tarragon, cumin, marjoram, salt, pepper and soy sauce. Simmer for 10 minutes.

Meanwhile, cook the vegeroni in boiling water for 8 to 10 minutes until done.

Add the cooked vegeroni to the tomato mixture. Mix well. Stir in the cheese. Simmer another 20 minutes, stirring occasionally.

Variation: The vegeroni and tomato mixture can also be placed in a casserole dish, sprinkled with wheat germ and grated Parmesan cheese and baked at 350°F (180°C) for 20 minutes.

*Available in bulk food stores.

Vegetarian Lasagne

This unusual lasagne lends itself to individual variations. The noodles do *not* need to be boiled for this dish.

PREPARATION TIME: 15 minutes
COOKING TIME: 30 minutes
YIELD: 4-6 servings

2 Tbsp	oil	25 mL
1	green pepper, chopped	1
2	onions, chopped	2
2	tomatoes, chopped	2
1 can (28-oz)	tomato sauce	1 can (796 mL)
8	lasagne noodles, uncooked	8
1 pkg (8-oz)	pressed cottage cheese	1 pkg (250 g)
3	eggs	3
1 tsp	garlic powder	5 mL
1 Tbsp	oregano	15 mL
1 Tbsp	basil	15 mL
2 cups	grated mozzarella cheese	500 mL

Preheat the oven to 350°F (180°C).

Sauté the green pepper, onions and tomatoes in the oil until soft. Spread half of the tomato sauce over the bottom of a 9-by-13 inch (4 L) baking dish. Place 4 lasagne noodles over the sauce.

Combine the cottage cheese, eggs, garlic powder, oregano and basil in a bowl until smooth. Spread over the noodles. Cover with the remaining noodles. Spread the sautéed vegetables on top. Cover with the remaining tomato sauce. Top with the grated mozzarella cheese. Bake uncovered for 30 minutes.

Serve with a tossed green salad and garlic bread.

Spicy Noodles

These noodles taste just like the ones served in your favourite Chinese restaurant.

PREPARATION TIME: **20 minutes**
YIELD: **4 servings**

8 oz	noodles (spaghetti or Chinese-style)	250 g
1/4 cup	light sesame oil*	50 mL
1/4 cup	light soy sauce*	50 mL
2 Tbsp	sesame paste*	25 mL
1 Tbsp	chili oil*	15 mL
1 Tbsp	vinegar	15 mL
2 tsp	minced fresh ginger root	10 mL
2 tsp	crushed Szechuan peppercorns*	10 mL
2 cloves	garlic, minced	2 cloves

Cook noodles according to package instructions. Drain and cool under cold water. Toss with 2 tablespoons (25 mL) sesame oil. Chill.

Stir together the soy sauce, sesame paste, remaining sesame oil, chili oil, vinegar, ginger, peppercorns and garlic. Pour the sauce over the noodles, toss and serve immediately.

Note: This dish may be served hot. After the noodles have been coated in the sauce, stir-fry in a frying pan or wok until heated through. Broccoli and/or snow peas may also be added.

*Available in Oriental food stores.

Neptune's Salmon Salad

The attractive and tasty combination of salmon and pasta creates a wonderful summer meal. Garnish with cherry tomatoes and serve with crusty bread.

PREPARATION TIME: **15** minutes
COOKING TIME: **10** minutes
REFRIGERATION TIME: **1** hour
YIELD: **4** servings

2 1/2 cups	medium bow pasta	625 mL
2 cans	salmon, drained and	2 cans
(7 3/4-oz)	broken up	(220 g)
1 1/4 cups	seeded and chopped	300 mL
	cucumber	
1/2 cup	chopped green pepper	125 mL
1 cup	plain yogurt	250 mL
1/4 cup	mayonnaise	50 mL
2 Tbsp	chopped green onion	25 mL
1 tsp	dill weed	5 mL
1/2 tsp	garlic powder	2 mL
1 tsp	marjoram	5 mL
1 tsp	seasoned salt	5 mL

Cook the pasta according to the package instructions. Drain and cool.

Combine the pasta, salmon, cucumber and green pepper in a serving bowl. Combine the yogurt, mayonnaise, green onion, dill weed, garlic powder, marjoram and seasoned salt in a separate bowl. Pour over the pasta mixture. Toss lightly to coat. Chill to blend flavours for at least 1 hour.

Shrimp Pasta Salad

A perfect summer buffet dish for a large crowd, this salad is best made the same day. It is most attractive served in a large white bowl.

PREPARATION TIME: **30 minutes**
COOKING TIME: **15 minutes**
YIELD: **20 servings**

6 cups	fusilli (corkscrew) pasta	1.5 L
1 pkg	frozen cooked Matane	1 pkg
(14-oz)	shrimp	(398 mL)
1 cup	olive oil	250 mL
6 cloves	garlic, crushed	6 cloves
1	red pepper	1
1	green pepper	1
8 oz	snow peas	250 g
1/2 cup	balsamic vinegar	125 mL
2 tsp	salt	10 mL
2 tsp	white pepper	10 mL

Cook the pasta in boiling salted water for 10 minutes or until 'al dente'. Drain and run cold water over the pasta. Dry on a tea towel. Place in a large serving bowl.

Defrost the shrimp and pat dry on paper towels. Add to the bowl of pasta. Combine 1/2 cup (125 mL) of the olive oil and the garlic. Toss into the pasta and shrimp. Allow to marinate while preparing the vegetables.

Cut the red and green peppers into 1-inch (2.5 cm) julienne strips. String and blanch the snow peas and pat dry on paper towel. Add the vegetables to the pasta.

Combine the remaining 1/2 cup (125 mL) olive oil with the balsamic vinegar, salt and pepper. Add to the pasta and toss.

Baked Spiced Rice

As an accompaniment to roast meats or chicken, this simple baked casserole is a winner.

PREPARATION TIME: **30 minutes**
COOKING TIME: **15-20 minutes**
YIELD: **4 servings**

1 cup	rice	250 mL
3 Tbsp	butter	45 mL
1	green onion, chopped	1
1 tsp	chervil	5 mL
1 tsp	curry powder or turmeric	5 mL
2 cups	chicken stock, hot	500 mL
1	bay leaf	1

Preheat the oven to 350°F (180°C).

Wash the rice. Melt the butter in a stove-to-oven casserole dish. Add the green onion and rice. Stir until the rice is glossy. Add the chervil and the spice of your choice. Add the hot stock and bay leaf. Bring to a boil. Cover and bake for 15 to 20 minutes.

No-Fry Fried Rice

You can eliminate the frying and still enjoy the flavour of fried rice.

PREPARATION TIME: **5 minutes**
COOKING TIME: **55 minutes**
YIELD: **8 servings**

2 cups	uncooked rice	500 mL
2 Tbsp	soy sauce	25 mL
1/4 cup	oil	50 mL
1 pkg	onion soup mix	1 pkg
(2 1/2-oz)		(66 g)
1	red or green pepper, sliced	1
1 can	water chestnuts, sliced	1 can
(8-oz)		(227 mL)
1 can	whole mushrooms	1 can
(10-oz)		(284 mL)
1 can	bamboo shoots	1 can
(8-oz)		(227 mL)
3 1/2 cups	liquid (from canned vegetables plus water as required)	875 mL

Preheat the oven to 350°F (180°C).

Combine all of the ingredients, stir together and place in a 2-quart (2 L) covered casserole.

Bake 55 minutes or until all of the liquid is absorbed.

Parsley-Pistachio Rice

The rich East Indian flavour of this dish makes it a fine complement to roast lamb.

PREPARATION TIME: **15** minutes
COOKING TIME: **30** minutes
YIELD: **6-8 servings**

2 cups	uncooked rice	500 mL
6 Tbsp	salted butter, cut up	90 mL
1 tsp	garlic salt	5 mL
1 tsp	onion salt	5 mL
6 Tbsp	chopped fresh parsley	90 mL
1/2 cup	chopped pistachio nuts	125 mL
1 tsp	white pepper	5 mL

Cook the rice according to package instructions.

Fluff the rice with a fork until all the grains have separated, adding the butter. Season with the garlic salt, onion salt and white pepper. Add the parsley and the nuts.

Note: This dish may be prepared in advance, but do not refrigerate. Reheat over low heat for 20 minutes, stirring frequently.

Risi e Bisi

This hearty vegetarian main course is our variation of an Italian classic.

PREPARATION TIME: 15 minutes
COOKING TIME: 45 minutes
YIELD: 2 servings

1 medium	onion, chopped	1 medium
1 Tbsp	butter	15 mL
1 cup	brown rice	250 mL
2 1/2 cups	water	625 mL
1	chicken bouillon cube	1
1 Tbsp	dry sherry	15 mL
1/2 tsp	pepper	2 mL
1 cup	frozen peas	250 mL
1 cup	grated Cheddar cheese	250 mL

Sauté the onion in the butter in a heavy saucepan for 3 to 4 minutes, until soft but not browned. Add the rice and stir to coat with the butter and onions. Add the water, bouillon cube, sherry and pepper. Cover and simmer for 40 minutes.

In the last 5 minutes, stir in the peas and continue cooking until tender. Stir in the cheese until melted. Serve immediately.

Wild Rice Casserole

Roll up your sleeves and let yourself get into it. This casserole is a warm and comforting dish that is a little bit out of the ordinary. Double the recipe to serve a crowd.

SOAKING TIME: overnight
PREPARATION TIME: 15 minutes
COOKING TIME: 45 minutes
YIELD: 6 servings

1 cup	wild rice	250 mL
2 Tbsp	oil	25 mL
2	onions, chopped	2
12 oz	lean ground beef	375 g
1 lb	Cheddar cheese, grated	500 g
1 can	tomatoes	1 can
(19-oz)		(540 mL)
1 can	mushroom pieces, drained	1 can
(10-oz)		(284 mL)
	salt and pepper to taste	

Rinse the rice and let it soak overnight in plenty of water. It will split open. Alternatively, the rice can be boiled for 30 minutes.

Preheat the oven to 350°F (180°C).

Heat the oil in a large frying pan. Sauté the onion with the beef until the pink disappears. Drain.

Put the cheese in a large bowl, reserving 1/2 cup (125 mL) for topping. Add the tomatoes, drained mushrooms and the salt and pepper. Drain the wild rice and add to the bowl. Add beef and onion to the bowl and mix thoroughly with your hands, breaking up the tomatoes, until completely blended.

Transfer the mixture to a casserole dish. Sprinkle the reserved cheese on top. Cover and bake for 45 minutes, removing the lid for the final 10 minutes.

Serve with a salad and crusty bread to round out the meal.

Tarragon Rice Salad

Rice salads are a colourful addition to any summer buffet table. The three recipes included here are each different and delicious. Tarragon spices up the vinaigrette in this recipe.

PREPARATION TIME: 20 minutes
COOKING TIME: 20 minutes
REFRIGERATION TIME: 4 hours
YIELD: 6 servings

1 cup	converted rice	250 mL
6 Tbsp	olive oil	90 mL
3 Tbsp	white or cider vinegar	45 mL
1 tsp	salt	5 mL
	freshly ground pepper to taste	
1 tsp	tarragon	5 mL
1/2 cup	chopped green or red pepper	125 mL
1/4 cup	finely chopped parsley	50 mL
1/4 cup	finely chopped onion	50 mL
1 cup	green peas, cooked and drained	250 mL
1 small	cucumber	1 small
	tomato wedges as garnish green and black olives as garnish	

Cook rice according to package instructions until tender but not mushy. While the rice cooks, combine the oil, vinegar, salt, pepper and tarragon.

After the rice is cooked but still warm, toss gently with the dressing. Cool. Fold in the pepper, parsley, onion and peas. Cover and refrigerate for at least 4 hours.

At serving time, pare the cucumber and cut lengthwise into 1/4-inch (5 mm) strips. Remove the seeds and cut the strips into 1/4-inch (5 mm) pieces. Toss with the rice mixture.

Pile the rice high on a platter. Surround with the tomato wedges and the green and black olives.

Curry and Rice Salad

Curry and raisins provide an Indian accent to this rice salad variation.

PREPARATION TIME: 30 minutes
YIELD: 4 servings

2 cups	cooked converted rice	500 mL
1	green pepper, cut into thin strips	1
1	red pepper, cut into thin strips	1
2-3 Tbsp	raisins or currants	25-45 mL
2 Tbsp	finely chopped parsley	25 mL
2-3	green onions, finely chopped	2-3
1/2 cup	oil	125 mL
1/3 cup	red wine vinegar	75 mL
1 Tbsp	lemon juice	15 mL
1 clove	garlic, crushed	1 clove
1 tsp	sugar	5 mL
dash	ground ginger	dash
1 Tbsp	curry powder	15 mL

Combine the rice, peppers, raisins, parsley and onions. Blend the remaining ingredients and pour over the rice mixture. Toss well.

Pineapple Rice Salad

This unusual rice salad can be spiced according to taste. Use more curry powder and dry mustard for spice lovers.

PREPARATION TIME: 15 minutes
REFRIGERATION TIME: 1 hour
YIELD: 6 servings

3 cups	cooked converted rice	750 mL
1 cup	chopped celery	250 mL
1/4 cup	chopped green pepper	50 mL
1/2 cup	pineapple chunks, drained	125 mL
3/4 cup	mayonnaise	175 mL
1 tsp	minced onion	5 mL
1 tsp	curry powder	5 mL
1/2 tsp	dry mustard	2 mL
	salt and freshly ground pepper to taste	

Combine ingredients. Cover and refrigerate for at least 1 hour before serving.

VEGETABLES

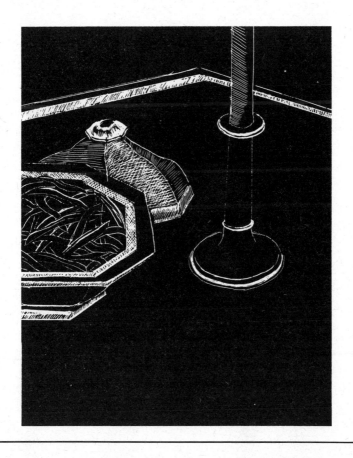

Asparagus Casserole

Plan a brunch around this super dish or take it to your next potluck. Either way it's a hit.

PREPARATION TIME: **20 minutes**
COOKING TIME: **10 minutes**
YIELD: **6 servings**

6	eggs	6
2 cans	asparagus tips	2 cans
(12-oz)		(341 mL)
1/4 cup	butter	50 mL
1/4 cup	flour	50 mL
1/2 cup	milk	125 mL
1/2 tsp	Worcestershire sauce	2 mL
2 Tbsp	chopped fresh parsley	25 mL
1/4 tsp	nutmeg	1 mL
dash	salt	dash
2/3 cup	bread crumbs	150 mL
1/4 cup	grated Parmesan cheese	50 mL
1/2 tsp	basil	2 mL
dash	cayenne pepper	dash

Preheat the oven to 400°F (200°C).

Hard-boil the eggs.

Drain the asparagus tips, reserving the liquid.

Melt the butter and stir in the flour. Cook for 1 minute. Add enough milk to the asparagus liquid to make 2 cups (500 mL). Stir into pan and add the Worcestershire sauce, parsley, nutmeg and salt. Cook, stirring frequently, until the sauce thickens.

Slice the eggs. Combine the asparagus, eggs and sauce in a casserole dish. Combine the bread crumbs, cheese, basil and cayenne and spread on top of the casserole. Bake for 10 minutes.

This is good served with smoked fish or ham and fresh bread or rolls.

Green Beans in Almond-Mustard Sauce

Dijon mustard provides a new zing to the ever-popular combination of green beans and almonds.

PREPARATION TIME: **10 minutes**
COOKING TIME: **10 minutes**
YIELD: **4-6 servings**

2 1/2 cups	whole green beans	625 mL
2 Tbsp	butter	25 mL
2 Tbsp	slivered unblanched almonds	25 mL
1 1/2 tsp	Dijon mustard	7 mL
1 tsp	salt	5 mL
pinch	freshly ground pepper	pinch

Cook the whole beans in a small quantity of boiling salted water until crisp-tender. While the beans cook, melt the butter in a small frying pan. Add the almonds and sauté over low heat until lightly browned. Stir in the mustard, salt and pepper and keep warm until the beans are cooked. Drain the beans and toss with the sauce.

Sesame Green Beans

Sesame seeds add crunch to these tangy green beans, delicious served hot or cold.

PREPARATION TIME: 15 minutes
COOKING TIME: 7 minutes
YIELD: 4-6 servings

1 lb	fresh green beans	500 g
1/4 cup	vinegar	50 mL
1/3 cup	olive oil	75 mL
1 1/2 tsp	oregano	7 mL
3/4 tsp	basil	3 mL
3/4 tsp	garlic salt	3 mL
1/4 cup	sesame seeds, toasted	50 mL
1/2 cup	grated Parmesan cheese	125 mL

Wash and trim the green beans. Steam until tender. Drain and put in a serving bowl. In a small bowl, combine the vinegar, oil, oregano, basil and garlic salt. Pour over the beans and toss. Stir in the sesame seeds and cheese.

Note: To toast sesame seeds, place them on a tray and broil for 3 to 5 minutes.

Broccoli Casserole

Rich, cheesy and crisp, this casserole transforms a simple meal.

PREPARATION TIME: 25 minutes
COOKING TIME: 35 minutes
YIELD: 6 servings

1 large	bunch of broccoli, cut into 2-inch (5 cm) pieces	1 large
3 Tbsp	oil	45 mL
4 medium	onions, sliced	4 medium
4 oz	mozzarella cheese, grated	125 g
1 can (10-oz)	cream of mushroom soup	1 can (284 mL)
1/2 cup	milk	125 mL
1 tsp	Worcestershire sauce	5 mL
4 oz	Cheddar cheese, grated	125 mL
	pepper to taste	
1 can (3-oz)	Durkee's Real French Fried Onions*	1 can (74 g)
dash	cayenne pepper	dash

Preheat the oven to 375°F (190°C).

Steam the broccoli until tender-crisp. Set aside. Heat the oil in a large frying pan. Sauté the onions until golden brown. Transfer to a casserole dish. Cover with the broccoli and then the mozzarella cheese. Combine the soup, milk and the Worcestershire sauce and pour over the mixture in casserole dish. Sprinkle with the Cheddar cheese and a little pepper. Top with the fried onions and a sprinkling of cayenne pepper.

Bake the casserole covered for 20 minutes and then uncovered for 15 minutes.

*Available in kosher food section or specialty food stores.

Braised Broccoli

Broccoli becomes sophisticated with the addition of gin or cognac.

PREPARATION TIME: **5** minutes
COOKING TIME: **10** minutes
YIELD: **4** servings

1 large	bunch of broccoli	1 large
3 Tbsp	oil	45 mL
2	green onions, chopped	2
2 Tbsp	soy sauce	25 mL
1 Tbsp	gin or cognac	15 mL
1 Tbsp	sugar	15 mL
1/4 cup	boiling water	50 mL

Remove the tough ends of the broccoli. Cut the broccoli into 1-inch (2.5 cm) slices.

Heat the oil in a frying pan. Sauté the green onions and broccoli for 5 minutes.

Combine the soy sauce, gin, sugar and water. Pour over the broccoli. Cover and cook over low heat for 5 minutes.

Sweet and Sour Red Cabbage

The red cabbage becomes an incredible shade of purple after cooking; it goes well with hearty meats such as pork, sausage or Wiener schnitzel.

PREPARATION TIME: **10 minutes**
COOKING TIME: **30 minutes**
YIELD: **6 servings**

3 Tbsp	shortening	45 mL
1 head	red cabbage, shredded	1 head
2 Tbsp	grated onion	25 mL
1 medium	apple, peeled and chopped	1 medium
2 tsp	salt	10 mL
2 tsp	caraway seeds	10 mL
1 Tbsp	brown sugar	15 mL
3 Tbsp	white vinegar	45 mL

Melt the shortening in a large saucepan. Add the cabbage, onion, apple and salt. Sprinkle in the caraway seeds and brown sugar. Mix together and cook, covered, over low to medium heat for 30 minutes. Add the vinegar and mix well. Add extra sugar to taste.

Carrots in Wine

This recipe gives the humble carrot a beauty treatment. Even children will eat cooked carrots when prepared this way.

PREPARATION TIME: 5 minutes
COOKING TIME: 10-15 minutes
YIELD: 2 servings

1 Tbsp	butter	15 mL
1/3 cup	white wine	75 mL
1 clove	garlic, peeled	1 clove
2 large *or* 4 small	carrots, peeled and cut into sticks	2 large *or* 4 small
	juice of 1/2 orange	
pinch	salt	pinch
	freshly ground pepper	
	cayenne pepper	

Combine the butter, wine and whole garlic clove in a small heavy saucepan and simmer for 5 minutes. Add the carrots, orange juice and salt. Cover and simmer gently until tender, adding a bit more wine if required. The liquid should reduce to a light glaze by the time the carrots are done. (If it hasn't, uncover the pan and raise the heat to reduce it quickly.) Remove the garlic clove and season with a good quantity of pepper and a whiff of cayenne.

Lemon Glazed Carrots

Create a terrific side dish with the following recipe.

PREPARATION TIME: 10 minutes
COOKING TIME: 20 minutes
YIELD: 4 servings

1 1/4 lb	carrots, peeled and thinly sliced	625 g
1 tsp	salt	5 mL
1/4 cup	butter or margarine	50 mL
1/4 cup	sugar	50 mL
1 tsp	grated lemon rind	5 mL
1 Tbsp	lemon juice	15 mL
	parsley as garnish	

Place the carrots in a medium saucepan containing 1 inch (2.5 cm) of boiling salted water. Cover and boil over medium heat for 10 minutes. Drain and set aside.

Melt the butter in a large frying pan over medium heat. Add the sugar and stir until it is dissolved. Stir in the lemon rind and lemon juice.

Add the carrots to the frying pan and cook, stirring frequently, until the carrots are glazed and the butter mixture is reduced. Sprinkle with parsley.

Note: Grated orange peel and orange juice may be substituted for the lemon.

Cauliflower Soufflé

Tired of the classic cauliflower with cheese sauce? If so, try this different version of cauliflower with cheese.

PREPARATION TIME: **15 minutes**
COOKING TIME: **40 minutes**
YIELD: **4 servings**

1 small	cauliflower	1 small
4 oz	butter	125 g
2 Tbsp	flour	25 mL
4	eggs, separated	4
1/2 pt	sour cream	250 mL
1/4 cup	grated Parmesan cheese	50 mL
	salt and freshly ground	
	pepper to taste	
pinch	nutmeg	pinch

Preheat the oven to 350°F (180°C).

Boil or steam the cauliflower until soft, about 8 to 10 minutes. Break into a buttered 8-by-5 inch (1.5 L) loaf pan.

Melt the butter. Remove from the heat and add the flour, lightly beaten egg yolks, sour cream and all but 2 tablespoons (25 mL) of the cheese. Beat the egg whites until very stiff. Fold into the cheese mixture. Add the salt, pepper and nutmeg. Pour over the cauliflower. Top with remaining Parmesan cheese.

Bake on the bottom rack for 5 minutes. Transfer to the middle rack and bake for 30 to 35 minutes more.

This soufflé is particularly good served with ham.

Red Hot Cauliflower

This dish works equally well with cauliflower alone or combined with broccoli.

PREPARATION TIME: **10** minutes
COOKING TIME: **25** minutes
YIELD: **4-6** servings

1 medium	cauliflower	1 medium
1/4	lemon	1/4
2-3 Tbsp	olive oil	25-45 mL
1/2 large	red pepper, diced	1/2 large
1/2 tsp	dried chili pepper flakes	2 mL
	salt to taste	
	chopped fresh parsley as garnish	

Divide the cauliflower into large florets. Steam until just tender, approximately 10 minutes. Remove to a kitchen towel to cool. Squeeze the juice of the lemon on top of the cauliflower while it is still hot. (This step may be done up to 1 hour ahead of time.)

Cover the bottom of a large frying pan with a film of olive oil. Cook the red pepper with the dried chili pepper flakes for 10 minutes over low heat.

Break the cauliflower into individual florets. Raise the heat to moderate, add the cauliflower to the pan and cook, stirring, until heated through. Add salt to taste and garnish with the parsley.

Curried Chick Peas

Try this unusual recipe as part of an Indian meal. It also works well as an appetizer, but be sure to pass around lots of paper napkins.

PREPARATION TIME: 5 minutes
COOKING TIME: 15 minutes
YIELD: 4 servings

1 large	onion, finely chopped	1 large
2 Tbsp	oil	25 mL
1 tsp	coriander	5 mL
1/2 tsp	chilies, dried and crushed	2 mL
1/2 tsp	ground cumin	2 mL
dash	ground cardamon	dash
1/2 tsp	black pepper	2 mL
1/4 tsp	cinnamon	1 mL
1 can	chick peas	1 can
(19-oz)		(540 mL)

Fry the onions in the oil, covered, over medium heat until golden. Add the spices and cook for 2 minutes, stirring frequently to keep from scorching.

Drain the chick peas, reserving the liquid, and add to the pan. Mix thoroughly with the onions and spices. Continue cooking for 3 minutes, stirring carefully from time to time. Add just enough liquid to keep the chick peas from sticking and cover the pan. Cook for approximately 10 more minutes, stirring once. When done, the chick peas should be almost dry and very soft.

Eggplant Boats

The little bit of extra effort required to prepare this dish results in an interesting presentation.

PREPARATION TIME: 20 minutes
COOKING TIME: 30 minutes
YIELD: 2 large servings

1 (1-lb)	eggplant	1 (500 g)
1/4 cup	chopped mushrooms	50 mL
1/4 cup	chopped green pepper	50 mL
1/4 cup	grated Parmesan cheese	50 mL
1/2 cup	tomato sauce	125 mL
1/2 tsp	salt	2 mL
1/2 tsp	oregano	2 mL
1/2 tsp	garlic powder	2 mL

Preheat the oven to 350°F (180°C).

Halve eggplant and remove the pulp, leaving a 1/4-inch (5 mm) thick shell. Steam the shells in 1/2 inch (1 cm) of water in a covered saucepan for approximately 7 minutes, or until slightly softened.

Dice the eggplant pulp and combine with the remaining ingredients in a medium bowl. Mound the mixture into the eggplant shells. Place in a shallow baking dish filled with 1/2 inch (1 cm) of water. Bake for 30 minutes, or until the eggplant mixture is tender.

Serve as a vegetarian main course with rice or pasta or as an accompaniment to broiled or barbecued meat.

Eggplant Casserole

Pine nuts add a unique taste and texture to this recipe.

PREPARATION TIME: 15 minutes
COOKING TIME: 40 minutes
YIELD: 4 servings

1 lb	eggplant, peeled and cubed	500 g
1 Tbsp	butter	15 mL
1-2 cloves	garlic, finely chopped	1-2 cloves
	salt and pepper to taste	
1/2 tsp	oregano	2 mL
1/2 tsp	thyme	2 mL
1 can	tomatoes, drained and	1 can
(14-oz)	chopped	(398 mL)
1 Tbsp	honey	15 mL
2 Tbsp	grated Parmesan cheese	25 mL
1 oz	pine nuts	28 g

Preheat the oven to 375°F (190°C).

Blanch the eggplant cubes in boiling salted water for 5 minutes. Drain well.

Arrange the eggplant in a greased shallow casserole dish. Dot with butter and sprinkle with the garlic, salt, pepper, oregano and thyme. Pour the chopped tomatoes and then the honey on top. Cover and bake for 20 minutes. Sprinkle with the Parmesan cheese and pine nuts. Bake uncovered for 20 more minutes, or until browned.

Serve with roast lamb and a Greek salad for a real Greek feast.

Eggplant Provençale

Eggplant Provençale, a cross between Ratatouille and Eggplant Parmesan, is delicious served either hot or cold.

PREPARATION TIME: 30 minutes
SITTING TIME: 30-60 minutes
COOKING TIME: 30 minutes
YIELD: 4 servings

1 large	eggplant	1 large
	oil as needed	
1 medium	cooking onion, chopped	1 medium
1	green pepper, chopped	1
2 cloves	garlic, chopped	2 cloves
	freshly ground pepper to taste	
1 can (32-oz)	tomatoes	1 can (909 mL)
1 can (5 1/2-oz)	tomato paste	1 can (156 mL)
2 Tbsp	fresh basil	25 mL
8 oz	mozzarella cheese, cut in pieces	250 g
1/2 cup	grated Parmesan cheese	125 mL

Peel the eggplant and cut into 1-inch (2 cm) cubes. Place in a colander over a bowl and salt lightly. Let the eggplant stand for 1/2 to 1 hour. Dry the eggplant thoroughly by pressing and squeezing it.

Place the oil, eggplant, onion, green pepper and garlic in a large frying pan. Sauté until the eggplant is golden. Add freshly ground pepper to taste.

Add the tomatoes, tomato paste, basil and mozzarella cheese. Simmer gently until the eggplant is tender and the mixture has thickened. Stir regularly. Sprinkle with the Parmesan cheese just before serving.

Ratatouille

Summer vegetables have never tasted better! Serve this tasty vegetable stew hot with crusty French bread or try it cold the next day.

PREPARATION TIME: 10 minutes
COOKING TIME: 45 minutes
YIELD: 4 servings

1 medium	eggplant	1 medium
1/4 cup	olive oil	50 mL
1 medium	onion, sliced	1 medium
1 clove	garlic, cut in half lengthwise	1 clove
3 medium	zucchini, sliced	3 medium
1/2	green pepper, sliced (optional)	1/2
3 large	tomatoes, sliced	3 large
1 tsp	basil	5 mL
1 tsp	oregano	5 mL
1/2 tsp	salt	2 mL
1/2 tsp	pepper	2 mL
2 tsp	Worcestershire sauce	10 mL
1/2 cup	grated Cheddar cheese	125 mL
1/4 cup	bread crumbs (optional)	50 mL

Wipe the eggplant and slice it lengthwise into 4 slices. Remove a strip of the peel from the end slices. Lay the pieces flat on paper towelling so they will drain.

In a large heavy frying pan, using 1 tablespoon (15 mL) of oil, sauté the onion and garlic until limp. Remove from the pan and reserve. Add the zucchini, pepper, and tomato slices. Sauté until soft. Remove and reserve with the onions. Gently sauté the eggplant, adding the remaining oil gradually, as required. Add the reserved vegetables. Cover immediately and reduce the heat. Simmer 10 minutes. Add the seasonings. Cook for an additional 20 minutes, stirring occasionally. Stir again at the end, breaking up the eggplant pieces.

Sprinkle with the cheese and crumbs. Cover and remove from the heat. Let stand for a few minutes to allow the cheese to melt.

Onions with Vermouth

This is a substantial vegetable side dish; its sweet flavour complements roast duck or other game.

PREPARATION TIME: 10 minutes
COOKING TIME: 40 minutes
YIELD: 6 servings

2-3 Tbsp	virgin olive oil	25-45 mL
12 medium	onions, peeled and quartered	12 medium
1 1/2 Tbsp	sugar	20 mL
1/4 cup	white vinegar	50 mL
3	firm, ripe tomatoes, peeled and chopped	3
2 cloves	garlic, minced	2 cloves
1	bay leaf	1
1/2 tsp	whole black peppercorns, crushed	2 mL
1/2 tsp	whole coriander seeds, crushed	2 mL
3/4 cup	dry vermouth	175 mL
1/4 cup	chopped fresh parsley	50 mL
	salt to taste	

Heat 2 tablespoons (25 mL) of the olive oil in a large frying pan over medium heat. Add the onions and sprinkle with the sugar. Cook, stirring, until the onions are soft, not brown, about 5 to 10 minutes. (Add the remainder of the olive oil if necessary.)

Add the vinegar, increase the heat and stir vigorously until the liquid is syrupy. Add the tomatoes, garlic, bay leaf, peppercorns, coriander and vermouth. Cook about 30 minutes, until the liquid is thick. Add the parsley and salt. Serve immediately.

Parsnip and Cress Purée

Delicious, nutritious, pretty, easy to do. . . and it can be prepared ahead of time. What more can one ask of a vegetable?

PREPARATION TIME: 20 minutes
COOKING TIME: 20 minutes
YIELD: 4 servings

1 1/2 lb	parsnips, peeled	750 g
1 bunch	watercress	1 bunch
2 Tbsp	butter	25 mL
as needed	milk or 10% cream	as needed
	salt and freshly ground	
	black pepper	

Cut parsnips into roughly equal chunks. Cook in boiling salted water to cover until tender (about 10 to 15 minutes). Drain well.

Meanwhile, pick over the washed cress, discarding any yellowed leaves and coarse stems. Blanch the leaves and tender stems in boiling water for barely 3 minutes. Drain through a sieve, cool briefly under running water, then squeeze dry.

Combine the parsnips and cress (in batches if necessary) in a blender or in the bowl of a food processor fitted with the steel blade. Add the butter in bits and blend or process until puréed, adding a little milk or cream to get the desired consistency. Season with salt and pepper. Serve hot.

Note: If this dish is not going to be served immediately, cool, then scrape into a bowl, cover and refrigerate. To reheat, transfer to a heavy saucepan and warm gently or spread in a shallow, buttered casserole dish, cover and reheat at 300°F (150°C) for 30 minutes.

Tipsy Squash

Be careful not to spill the liquid when serving the squash; you won't want to lose any of the sauce.

PREPARATION TIME: **10 minutes**
COOKING TIME: **45 minutes**
YIELD: **2 servings**

1	acorn squash	1
1/4 cup	Grand Marnier	50 mL
2 Tbsp	butter	25 mL
2 tsp	brown sugar	10 mL
1/2 tsp	nutmeg	2 mL

Preheat the oven to 350°F (180°C).

Cut the squash in half. Remove the seeds and fibres from the cavity. Place the squash skin side down in a shallow baking dish containing 1/2 inch (1 cm) of water. In each cavity, place half of the liqueur, butter, brown sugar and nutmeg.

Bake for 45 minutes, or until soft.

Sweet Potato Surprise

This dish is a great accompaniment to Thanksgiving turkey.

PREPARATION TIME: 15 minutes
COOKING TIME: 25 minutes
YIELD: 8 servings

2 cans (19-oz)	sweet potatoes	2 cans (540 mL)
1/3 cup	brown sugar	75 mL
1 1/2 Tbsp	cornstarch	20 mL
1 tsp	cinnamon	5 mL
dash	nutmeg	dash
2 Tbsp	butter	25 mL
1 tsp	lemon juice	5 mL
1 can (10-oz)	mandarin oranges	1 can (284 mL)
1/2 cup	orange juice (approximately) toasted slivered almonds as garnish	125 mL

Preheat the oven to 375°F (190°C).

Drain the sweet potatoes and lay them in a greased dish.

Combine the brown sugar, cornstarch, cinnamon, nutmeg, butter and lemon juice in a saucepan. Drain the oranges, reserving the liquid. Add the reserved liquid plus orange juice to equal 1 cup (250 mL) to the saucepan. Cook and stir over medium heat until boiling.

Pour the sauce over the sweet potatoes and bake for 25 minutes. Add the mandarin oranges during the final minutes of baking. Sprinkle with toasted slivered almonds.

Quick 'n' Easy Meatless Chili

This chili makes a satisfying vegetarian meal served with rice. Prepare a day ahead to let the flavours mingle.

PREPARATION TIME: 20 minutes
COOKING TIME: 15 minutes
YIELD: 4 servings

2 Tbsp	oil	25 mL
2 large	onions, chopped	2 large
2	green peppers, chopped	2
2 cloves	garlic, chopped	2 cloves
1 can	tomatoes	1 can
(28-oz)		(796 mL)
1 can	kidney beans	1 can
(19-oz)		(540 mL)
2 tsp	chili powder	10 mL
1/2 tsp	ground cumin	2 mL
1/2 cup	cashew pieces	125 mL

Heat the oil in a large frying pan. Add the onions, green peppers and garlic and sauté until soft. Add the tomatoes and their liquid, and continue to cook.

Drain the kidney beans and rinse. Add to the frying pan and stir. Add the chili powder and cumin.

Simmer for 15 minutes.

Just before serving, add cashew pieces and mix through.

Curried Fruit

Complement any pork entrée with this unique side dish. Yes, the recipe does require 3 to 4 *tablespoons* of curry powder.

PREPARATION TIME: **10 minutes**
COOKING TIME: **45 minutes**
YIELD: **4-6 servings**

1/3 cup	butter	75 mL
2/3 cup	brown sugar	150 mL
3-4 Tbsp	curry powder	40-50 mL
1 can (14-oz)	peaches	1 can (398 mL)
1 can (14-oz)	pears	1 can (398 mL)
1 can (14-oz)	pineapple chunks	1 can (398 mL)
1 can (10-oz)	tangerine segments	1 can (284 mL)
1 can (14-oz)	apricots	1 can (398 mL)

Preheat the oven to 350°F (180°C).

Melt the butter in a saucepan. Add the brown sugar and curry powder. Cook until the sugar is completely dissolved.

Drain the fruit. Place in a large casserole. Pour the brown sugar mixture over the fruit. Cover and bake for 45 minutes.

SALADS

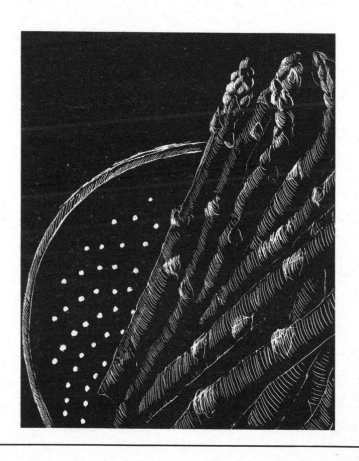

Avocado-Crab Salad

Elegant as an appetizer, stunning as part of a cold plate arrangement, this salad is refreshing, quick and easy.

PREPARATION TIME: 15 minutes
YIELD: 4 servings

2	avocados	2
2 cans	snow-crab meat	2 cans
(6-oz) *or*		(170 g) *or*
1 1/2 cups	fresh crab meat	375 mL
2 Tbsp	mayonnaise	25 mL
	juice of 1 lemon	
dash	pepper	dash
dash	paprika	dash
8	romaine lettuce leaves	8
	as garnish	
several	fresh shrimp, deveined,	several
	cooked and cooled	
	(optional)	

Slice the avocados in half, discarding the pits. Scoop out about a teaspoonful of flesh from each half. Combine this with the crab, mayonnaise, lemon juice, pepper and paprika. Fill the avocado halves with the crab mixture and serve on a bed of romaine lettuce. Shrimp may be arranged on top.

Variation: This recipe can easily be halved for a delicious start to an intimate candlelight dinner.

Esoteric Greens

This attractive and tasty marinated salad is a little bit out of the ordinary. If you are not familiar with the versatile leek, you will be pleasantly surprised.

PREPARATION TIME: 30 minutes
MARINATING TIME: overnight
YIELD: 6 servings

3	leeks, white parts only	3
1 can (14-oz)	artichoke hearts, drained and rinsed	1 can (398 mL)
1/2 cup	oil	125 mL
	juice of 1 lemon	
1 Tbsp	Dijon mustard	15 mL
pinch	cayenne pepper	pinch
pinch	salt	pinch
1	avocado	1
1/4 cup	coarsely chopped fresh parsley	50 mL
1 Tbsp	capers (optional)	15 mL

Cut leeks in half lengthwise and rinse carefully. Cut crosswise into 2-inch (5 cm) lengths and blanch for two minutes in a steamer over boiling water. Run under cold water. Drain and transfer to a sealed refrigerator container. Cut artichoke hearts into quarters and add to leeks.

Whisk together the oil, lemon juice, mustard and seasonings. Taste marinade and adjust seasonings if desired. Spoon the marinade over the vegetables and refrigerate overnight.

Just before serving, cut the avocado into bite size pieces and toss gently with the leeks. Transfer the salad to a serving platter. Sprinkle with the chopped parsley and capers.

Red and Green Salad

Serve this delectable salad in a white ceramic dish for maximum impact.

PREPARATION TIME: 15-20 minutes
COOKING TIME: 4-5 minutes
YIELD: 4 servings

Salad

1 lb	green beans	500 g
1	red pepper	1

Vinaigrette

3 Tbsp	red wine vinegar	45 mL
2 tsp	Dijon mustard	10 mL
1 clove	garlic, minced	1 clove
1 tsp	basil	5 mL
1/2 tsp	sugar	2 mL
1/2 tsp	salt	2 mL
1/3 cup	vegetable or olive oil	75 mL

Salad: Trim the ends off the beans and cook in boiling water for 4 to 5 minutes, or until tender-crisp. Cool under cold water and drain well. Cover and refrigerate.

Remove the seeds from the pepper; cut into thin strips.

Vinaigrette: In a food processor or a jar with a tight-fitting lid, combine the ingredients for the vinaigrette. Process or shake until well blended. Pour over the pepper strips and toss gently. Refrigerate. Before serving, add the green beans and toss again.

Variation: Thin slices of red onion may be sprinkled on top to give this salad an extra 'bite'.

Dijon Salad

The bite of Dijon, the crunch of water chestnuts and the splash of colour combine to make this salad special.

PREPARATION TIME: 5 minutes
YIELD: 4 servings

Salad

2 heads	Boston lettuce	2 heads
1	red pepper	1
8-10	water chestnuts	8-10

Dressing

3 cloves	garlic, finely chopped	3 cloves
2 Tbsp	white wine vinegar	25 mL
1 1/2 Tbsp	Dijon mustard	20 mL
	salt to taste	
	freshly ground pepper to taste	
6 Tbsp	olive oil	75 mL

Salad: Wash the lettuce and tear into pieces. Slice the red pepper lengthwise into matchsticks. Thinly slice the water chestnuts. Toss these ingredients together.

Dressing: Combine the garlic, vinegar, mustard, salt and pepper. Whisk in the oil, 1 tablespoon (15 mL) at a time.

Pour over salad and toss.

Variation: Substitute tarragon vinegar for white wine vinegar.

Tabbouleh

This is a refreshing, tasty Middle Eastern salad that is also both inexpensive and nutritious.

SOAKING TIME: **2 hours**
PREPARATION TIME: **25 minutes**
YIELD: **10 servings**

Salad

1 cup	bulgur wheat*	250 mL
4 cups	boiling water	1 L
1 large	bunch of parsley	1 large
1/2 cup	fresh mint	125 mL
or 3 Tbsp	dried mint	or 45 mL
6-8	green onions	6-8
2 large	tomatoes	2 large

Dressing

1/3 cup	lemon juice	75 mL
1/4 cup	vegetable oil	50 mL
2 tsp	salt	10 mL
1/2 tsp	cinnamon	2 mL
dash	pepper	dash

Salad: Put the bulgur wheat into a large bowl. Add the boiling water and cover. Let stand for 2 hours, or until the wheat puffs up. Drain thoroughly in a strainer and pat dry with a paper towel.

Chop the parsley, mint, green onions and tomatoes. Add to the wheat.

Dressing: Combine the ingredients and add to the salad. Mix well. Refrigerate.

This salad tastes even better the next day when the flavours have blended. Serve it as a side salad or with pieces of pita bread as a dip.

*Available in bulk food and health food stores.

Cucumber Salad

Cool your palate with our cucumber salad.

PREPARATION TIME: 15 minutes
REFRIGERATION TIME: 8 hours
YIELD: 6 servings

1/2 cup	mayonnaise	125 mL
1/2 tsp	salt	2 mL
1/4 tsp	celery seed	1 mL
dash	pepper	dash
2 medium	cucumbers, thinly sliced	2 medium
1 small	onion, thinly sliced	1 small

Combine all the ingredients.

Cover and refrigerate for 8 hours. Do not refrigerate more than 24 hours.

Tomato-Cucumber Raita

For an antidote to Indian or other spicy food, serve this refreshing salad.

PREPARATION TIME: **10 minutes**
REFRIGERATION TIME: **1 hour**
YIELD: **4 servings**

1 medium	cucumber, peeled	1 medium
3/4 tsp	salt	3 mL
1 medium	firm tomato	1 medium
2 Tbsp	finely chopped onion	25 mL
2 1/2 tsp	ground coriander	12 mL
1/2 cup	plain yogurt	125 mL
1 tsp	ground cumin	5 mL

Slice the cucumber into four lengthwise strips. Scrape out the seeds and discard. Chop remaining pulp. Sprinkle with salt and set aside for 5 minutes, then gently squeeze to remove any excess liquid.

Cut the tomato into 1/2-inch (1 cm) cubes.

Combine the cucumber, tomato, onion and coriander. Blend the yogurt and cumin and coat the vegetable mixture. Cover and refrigerate for 1 hour or until well chilled.

French Tomato Salad

When artfully arranged, French Tomato Salad can form the centrepiece of a light summer luncheon.

PREPARATION TIME: **10 minutes**
YIELD: **4 servings**

4	tomatoes, firm and ripe	4
1/2	red pepper, thinly sliced	1/2
2-3	green onions, chopped	2-3
1 tsp	coarsely chopped fresh dill	5 mL
	salt and pepper	
1/4-1/2 cup	extra virgin olive oil	50-125 mL
2 Tbsp	balsamic vinegar	25 mL

Prepare the tomatoes by slicing off the tops and bottoms. Place stem ends down and cut in half horizontally. Scoop out the pulp and juice from each half. Slice into thin rounds.

Arrange the tomatoes on a glass or white plate. Arrange the sliced red pepper on top and sprinkle with the green onions, dill, salt and pepper. Combine the oil and vinegar. Drizzle over the vegetables.

Potato Salad Piquant

Add zest to your next meal with this unusual potato salad.

PREPARATION TIME: **40 minutes**
REFRIGERATION TIME: **6 hours**
YIELD: **8 servings**

8	new potatoes, scrubbed	8
1/3 cup	olive oil	75 mL
1/4 cup	white wine vinegar	50 mL
1 Tbsp	sugar	15 mL
1 tsp	salt	5 mL
3 drops	Tabasco sauce	3 drops
3	banana peppers, seeded and finely chopped	3
1/2 cup	slivered Spanish onion	125 mL
1 can (7-oz)	corn niblets	1 can (198 mL)
1 large	carrot, grated	1 large
1/2 cup	pitted and chopped green olives	125 mL

Boil the potatoes until just tender. Cool slightly.

Combine the remaining ingredients in a large bowl.

Coarsely chop the potatoes leaving the skin on. Add to the bowl and toss well, coating the potatoes well. Cover and refrigerate for 6 hours.

Red Potato and Asparagus Salad

For a pleasant change from mayonnaise-based potato salads, bring our version to your next picnic.

PREPARATION TIME: 15 minutes
COOKING TIME: 25 minutes
YIELD: 6 servings

2 lb small	red potatoes, unpeeled	1 kg small
1 cup	vegetable oil	250 mL
1/4 cup	red wine vinegar	50 mL
1/4 cup	finely chopped red onion	50 mL
3 Tbsp	finely chopped fresh dill	45 mL
1 Tbsp	Dijon mustard	15 mL
	salt and pepper to taste	
12 stalks	asparagus	12 stalks
2	eggs, hard-boiled and quartered	2

Cook the potatoes until just tender. Drain. Combine the oil, vinegar, onion, dill, mustard, salt and pepper. Pour the dressing over the warm potatoes and toss lightly. Refrigerate overnight, covered.

Cook the asparagus until crisp-tender. Cut into 2-inch (5 cm) pieces. Toss with the potatoes. Garnish with the eggs.

Variation: Substitute 1/2 pound (250 g) cooked green beans for the asparagus.

Mandarin Orange and Almond Salad

Tart and crunchy, this salad is also lovely to look at.

PREPARATION TIME: 15 minutes
COOKING TIME: 5 minutes
YIELD: 4 servings

1/2 tsp	salt	2 mL
dash	pepper	dash
1 Tbsp	sugar	15 mL
pinch	dried parsley	pinch
1/4 cup	red wine vinegar	50 mL
dash	Tabasco sauce	dash
	mixed spinach and lettuce greens	
1/4 cup	slivered almonds	50 mL
4 tsp	sugar	20 mL
1 can (10-oz)	mandarin oranges, drained	1 can (284 mL)

Combine the salt, pepper, sugar, parsley, vinegar and Tabasco. Mix well and chill. Wash and dry the salad greens.

To prepare the candied almond garnish, cook the almonds and sugar together over high heat, stirring constantly. When the sugar has melted, remove from the heat and continue stirring for 1 minute to prevent sticking. Spread thinly on an oiled cookie sheet.

Toss the prepared greens with the mandarin oranges and dressing. Sprinkle the candied almonds over the salad.

Wonderful Waldorf

Here is a salad appropriate for winter when lettuce and tomatoes are poor in quality and expensive.

PREPARATION TIME: **5-10 minutes**
YIELD: **4 servings**

Salad

1	red apple	1
1	green apple	1
2 stalks	celery	2 stalks
1/2 cup	chopped walnuts	125 mL
1/2 cup	almonds	125 mL
1/4 cup	raisins	50 mL
1/4 cup	sunflower seeds	50 mL

Dressing

1/2 cup	sour cream	125 mL
1/2 cup	mayonnaise	125 mL
1 tsp	lemon juice	5 mL

Salad: Cut the apples into quarters. Remove the cores and dice coarsely. Put in a large bowl. Slice in the celery. Add the walnuts, almonds, raisins and sunflower seeds.

Dressing: Combine the sour cream, mayonnaise and lemon juice. Add to the salad ingredients and toss well.

SAUCES AND DRESSINGS

Creamy Salad Dressing

This basic creamy salad dressing with an understated zip will become a staple of your salad repertoire.

PREPARATION TIME: **10 minutes**
YIELD: **3/4 cup (175 mL)**

1 tsp	beaten egg yolk	5 mL
2-3 tsp	Dijon mustard	10-15 mL
dash	Tabasco sauce	dash
1/2 tsp	finely chopped garlic	2 mL
	salt to taste	
	freshly ground pepper to taste	
1 tsp	white wine vinegar	5 mL
1/2 cup	olive oil	125 mL
1-2 tsp	fresh lemon juice	5-10 mL
1 tsp	35% cream	5 mL

Combine beaten egg yolk, mustard, Tabasco sauce, garlic, salt, pepper and vinegar.

Using a whisk, beat vigorously to blend the ingredients. Still beating, gradually add the oil. Beat until thick and well blended. Add the lemon juice and beat in the cream. Add more mustard, salt, pepper or lemon juice to taste.

Garlic Salad Dressing

If you are fond of garlic, you'll want this dressing on hand.

PREPARATION TIME: 10 minutes
YIELD: 3/4 cup (175 mL)

2 cloves	garlic, crushed	2 cloves
1 tsp	salt	5 mL
1 Tbsp	mayonnaise	15 mL
1 Tbsp	red wine vinegar	15 mL
1/2 cup	oil	125 mL
	juice of 1/2 lemon	
1 Tbsp	dried parsley	15 mL

Combine the garlic, salt and mayonnaise. Using a whisk, add the vinegar, oil, lemon juice and parsley. Mix well. Store in a covered container in the refrigerator.

Lemon-Sesame Dressing

The nutty flavour of toasted sesame seeds combines with the tartness of freshly-squeezed lemon juice to create an unusual salad dressing.

PREPARATION TIME: **10 minutes**
COOKING TIME: **3-4 minutes**
YIELD: **1/2 cup (125 mL)**

2 tsp	sesame seeds	10 mL
1/3 cup	vegetable oil	75 mL
	juice of 1 lemon	
2 tsp	sugar	10 mL
1/2 tsp	onion salt	2 mL

Preheat the oven to 350°F (180°C).

Toast the sesame seeds on a piece of foil for 3 to 4 minutes, or until golden.

Combine the remaining ingredients in a bottle. Add the toasted seeds and shake well.

This dressing is particularly good served on a mixed green salad.

Parmesan Dressing

Our testers particularly enjoyed this rich-tasting dressing; we recommend it on any basic green salad.

PREPARATION TIME: **5 minutes**
YIELD: **1 1/2 cups (375 mL)**

1/3 cup	cider vinegar	75 mL
2/3 cup	oil	150 mL
1 tsp	onion powder	5 mL
1 tsp	pepper	5 mL
1/4 tsp	salt	1 mL
2 tsp	dried basil	10 mL
2 Tbsp	grated Parmesan cheese	25 mL

Combine all ingredients. Store in a covered glass jar.

Honey Mustard

Our homemade version of the piquant but sweet mustards currently on the market provides the same gourmet taste without the specialty store price.

PREPARATION TIME: **5 minutes**
COOKING TIME: **5-10 minutes**
YIELD: **3/4 cup (175 mL)**

1/4 cup	honey	50 mL
1/2 cup	dry mustard	125 mL
1/2 cup	white vinegar	125 mL
1 Tbsp	corn oil	15 mL
1 tsp	salt	5 mL
1/4 tsp	allspice	1 mL
1/4 tsp	garlic powder	1 mL
1/4 tsp	white pepper	1 mL

Combine all the ingredients in a saucepan. Boil until thick, about 5 to 10 minutes, stirring constantly.

This mustard is excellent served with cold meats and cheese. It should be stored in the refrigerator in a glass jar.

Sweet Hot Mustard

As the following recipe illustrates, homemade mustard is quick and easy to prepare. You will have lots left over to give as gifts.

PREPARATION TIME: 5 minutes
COOKING TIME: 5 minutes
YIELD: 3 cups (750 mL)

3/4 cup	dry mustard	175 mL
3/4 cup	sugar	175 mL
1 Tbsp	flour	15 mL
1 tsp	salt	5 mL
2	eggs, beaten	2
1 cup	evaporated milk	250 mL
3/4 cup	white vinegar	175 mL

Combine the mustard, sugar, flour and salt. Gradually add the beaten eggs and milk. Slowly add the vinegar. Cook over medium heat until thickened.

Store in a glass jar in the refrigerator.

Mustard-Dill Sauce

Try serving this flavourful sauce with grilled fish or lamb. Its taste improves with time.

PREPARATION TIME: 10 minutes
YIELD: 1 1/2 cups (375 mL)

1/2 cup	Dijon or dark prepared mustard	125 mL
2 tsp	dry mustard	10 mL
1/4 cup	sugar	50 mL
1/4 cup	white vinegar	50 mL
2/3 cup	vegetable oil	150 mL
1/4 cup	finely chopped fresh dill salt to taste	50 mL

Combine the mustards and sugar in a mixing bowl. Stir in the vinegar with a wire whisk. Gradually add the oil, stirring rapidly with the whisk. Add the dill and salt.

Note: This sauce has a very thin consistency. Do not expect a mayonnaise-type result.

Oriental Marinade

Here is a versatile recipe which may be used for a marinade, dipping sauce or barbecue baste for red meat. It makes the less-expensive cuts of meat tender and flavourful.

PREPARATION TIME: 10 minutes
YIELD: 1 1/2 cups (375 mL)

1/2 cup	olive oil	125 mL
1/2 cup	soy sauce	125 mL
1/2 cup	sherry or Madeira	125 mL
1 Tbsp	freshly grated ginger root	15 mL
1 Tbsp	grated orange rind	15 mL

Combine all the ingredients.

If using as a marinade, marinate the meat for 2 to 3 hours prior to cooking.

Lamb and Pork Baste

Do not be put off by the taste of the uncooked sauce—it works miracles on barbecued or roasted meat.

PREPARATION TIME: 5 minutes
YIELD: 1/2-3/4 cup (125-175 mL)

2 Tbsp	white vinegar	25 mL
1/2 cup	white wine	125 mL
2 Tbsp	sugar	25 mL
1/2 tsp	basil	2 mL
1/2 tsp	rosemary	2 mL
1/2 tsp	thyme	2 mL
1/2 tsp	lemon pepper	2 mL
1/2 tsp	celery salt	2 mL
1/2 tsp	garlic powder	2 mL
1/2 tsp	ginger	2 mL
1/2 tsp	tarragon	2 mL

Combine all of the ingredients in a glass jar and shake well.

Use to baste barbecued or baked chops or roasts. Baste chops every 5 minutes; baste roasts every 15 minutes.

QUICK BREADS
AND MUFFINS

Grandma Mac's Scones

Grandma Mac is a 93-year-old woman who has been cooking for 80 years. This recipe came with her when she immigrated to Canada from Scotland in 1911.

PREPARATION TIME: 15 minutes
COOKING TIME: 10 minutes
YIELD: 12 large scones

2 cups	all-purpose flour	500 mL
1 Tbsp	sugar	15 mL
pinch	salt	pinch
2 tsp	baking powder	10 mL
1 tsp	baking soda	5 mL
1/2 tsp	cream of tartar	2 mL
2 Tbsp	margarine or butter	25 mL
1	egg, well-beaten	1
1 cup	buttermilk	250 mL
1/4 cup	butter, melted	50 mL

Preheat the oven to 425°F (220°C).

Sift together the flour, sugar, salt, baking powder, baking soda and cream of tartar. Blend in the margarine or butter by hand until fine crumbs are formed.

Beat together the egg and buttermilk and add to the above mixture. Blend until the dough is soft and pliable. (You may have to add a little more buttermilk to obtain the right consistency.)

Roll the dough as little as possible on a floured board to a thickness of 1/2 inch (1.25 cm). Cut the dough into rounds using the rim of a small juice glass. Place on an ungreased cookie sheet. Bake on the middle rack of the oven until the scones have risen and turned golden, approximately 10 minutes.

Remove from the oven and immediately brush the tops with the melted butter. Cover with a loose sheet of waxed paper to keep moist.

Serve with clotted cream and strawberry preserves.

Apple-Pecan Muffins

Try making these healthy muffins in the autumn when apples are at their most delicious.

PREPARATION TIME: 15 minutes
COOKING TIME: 25 minutes
YIELD: 2 dozen large muffins

1 1/2 cups	vegetable oil	375 mL
2 cups	sugar	500 mL
3	eggs	3
2 cups	all-purpose flour, sifted	500 mL
1 tsp	cinnamon	5 mL
1 tsp	nutmeg	5 mL
1 tsp	baking soda	5 mL
3/4 tsp	salt	3 mL
1 cup	whole wheat flour, sifted	250 g
1 cup	chopped pecans	250 g
3 cups	peeled, cored and chopped apples	750 mL
3 Tbsp	apple juice	45 mL
1 tsp	rum flavouring (optional)	5 mL

Preheat the oven to 375°F (190°C).

In a large bowl, beat the oil and sugar until thick and opaque. Add the eggs, one at a time, beating well after each addition.

Sift together the all-purpose flour, cinnamon, nutmeg, baking soda and salt. Add the whole wheat flour. Add to the egg mixture and mix until well blended.

Add the pecans, apples, apple juice and rum flavouring. Stir until the apples and nuts are evenly distributed. Fill large muffin tins lined with paper muffin cups. Bake for 25 minutes.

Apple Spice Muffins

Excellent for brunch or for a coffee break, these muffins resemble individual coffee cakes.

PREPARATION TIME: **20 minutes**
COOKING TIME: **15-20 minutes**
YIELD: **12 large muffins**

Muffins

2 cups	all-purpose flour	500 mL
3 1/2 tsp	baking powder	17 mL
1 tsp	cinnamon	5 mL
1 tsp	nutmeg	5 mL
1/2 tsp	salt	2 mL
1/2 cup	sugar	125 mL
1 cup	peeled and chopped apple	250 mL
1	egg, lightly beaten	1
1 cup	milk	250 mL
1/3 cup	butter or shortening, melted	75 mL

Topping

2 Tbsp	brown sugar	25 mL
1/4 tsp	cinnamon	1 mL
1/4 tsp	nutmeg	1 mL

Preheat the oven to 400°F (200°C).

Muffins: Sift together the flour, baking powder, cinnamon, nutmeg, salt and sugar. Add the chopped apple. Combine the egg, milk and butter or shortening. Add the wet ingredients to the dry ingredients. Do not overmix. Spoon into 12 large greased muffin tins.

Topping: Combine the sugar, cinnamon and nutmeg. Sprinkle the topping over the top of the batter.

Bake the muffins for 15 to 20 minutes.

Best Banana Muffins

The addition of bananas creates a moister and sweeter version of basic bran muffins.

PREPARATION TIME: 15 minutes
COOKING TIME: 20-25 minutes
YIELD: 12 muffins

1/2 cup	sugar	125 mL
1/4 cup	vegetable oil	50 mL
1 cup	mashed ripe banana	250 mL
1	egg, lightly beaten	1
1 tsp	vanilla extract	5 mL
1/2 cup	bran cereal	125 mL
1/2 cup	all-purpose flour	125 mL
1/2 cup	whole wheat flour	125 mL
1 tsp	baking powder	5 mL
1 tsp	baking soda	5 mL
1/2 tsp	salt	2 mL
1/2 cup	raisins	125 mL

Preheat the oven to 350°F (180°C).

Combine the sugar, oil, banana, egg, vanilla and bran cereal. Let stand 5 minutes.

Stir together the all-purpose and whole wheat flours, baking powder, baking soda and salt. Add to the bran mixture and stir until just combined. Fold in the raisins.

Spoon the batter into greased muffin tins, filling about 3/4 full.

Bake for 20 to 25 minutes, until golden brown.

Blueberry Cornmeal Muffins

Always tender and delicious, Blueberry Cornmeal Muffins will freeze well for another day. Wrap in foil and reheat for serving.

PREPARATION TIME: 15 minutes
COOKING TIME: 20-25 minutes
YIELD: 12 large muffins

1 cup	all-purpose flour	250 mL
1 cup	yellow cornmeal	250 mL
1/3 cup	sugar	75 mL
3 tsp	baking powder	15 mL
1/4 tsp	salt	1 mL
1 tsp	ground coriander	5 mL
1/2 tsp	grated lemon peel	2 mL
1 cup	milk	250 mL
1/3 cup	vegetable oil	75 mL
1	egg	1
1 cup	fresh blueberries	250 mL

Preheat the oven to 400°F (200°C).

Combine the flour, cornmeal, sugar, baking powder, salt, coriander and lemon peel. In a separate bowl combine the milk, oil and egg and beat lightly. Add the liquid to the dry ingredients and stir until just moistened. Quickly stir in the blueberries. Fill 12 large buttered muffin cups. (They can be filled level with the top since the batter does not rise a great deal.) Bake for 20 to 25 minutes, or until golden.

Serve warm.

Country Bran Muffins

Developed with friends during a leisurely country weekend, our muffin recipe yields a delightfully moist version of an old favourite. Serve warm if possible.

PREPARATION TIME: 10 minutes
COOKING TIME: 30-35 minutes
YIELD: 12 large muffins

1	egg	1
3/4 cup	brown sugar	175 mL
3/4 cup	vegetable oil	175 mL
1 1/2 cups	whole wheat flour	375 mL
1 cup	bran and wheat germ combined in any proportion	250 mL
1 tsp	baking soda	5 mL
1/2 tsp	salt	2 mL
1 cup	buttermilk	250 mL
1 cup	raisins	250 mL

Preheat the oven to 350°F (180°C).

Combine the egg, sugar and oil. Add all the remaining ingredients, stirring until just moistened. Place large paper baking cups in muffin tins and fill nearly to the top. Bake for 30 to 35 minutes.

Note: You may use 1/2 cup (125 mL) milk combined with 1/2 cup (125 mL) sour cream or yogurt as a substitute for the buttermilk.

Rich Molasses Buckwheat Muffins

Buckwheat groats can be found at your local health food store. They make a rich muffin, great for after-school snacks.

PREPARATION TIME: **10-15 minutes**
COOKING TIME: **20 minutes**
YIELD: **12 muffins**

1/4 cup	shortening	50 mL
3 Tbsp	sugar	45 mL
2 Tbsp	molasses	25 mL
1	egg	1
1 1/2 cups	sifted all-purpose flour	375 mL
2 tsp	baking powder	10 mL
1/2 tsp	baking soda	2 mL
1/2 tsp	salt	2 mL
3/4 cup	fine buckwheat groats	175 mL
1 cup	buttermilk	250 mL
1/4 cup	finely chopped raisins, pitted dates or nuts	50 mL

Preheat the oven to 425°F (220°C).

Cream the shortening until fluffy. Add the sugar and molasses and beat until light. Beat in the egg.

Sift together the flour, baking powder, baking soda and salt. Add to the creamed mixture. Add the groats and buttermilk, stirring only until the dry ingredients are moistened. Stir in the raisins, dates or nuts.

Grease large muffin tins. Fill 1/2 to 2/3 full. Bake muffins until they are brown on top, about 20 minutes.

Serve warm with butter and honey.

Chock-Full Muffins

If you like something sweet to start your day, try these terrific muffins. One is big enough for a light meal.

PREPARATION TIME: 20 minutes
COOKING TIME: 20 minutes
YIELD: 12 large muffins

1/4 cup	butter	50 mL
1/2 cup	packed brown sugar	125 mL
1/4 cup	honey	50 mL
2	eggs	2
1 1/4 cups	peanut butter	300 mL
1 1/4 cups	milk	300 mL
1 1/2 cups	bran	375 mL
1 cup	flour	250 mL
1 1/2 tsp	baking powder	7 mL
1/2 tsp	baking soda	2 mL
3/4 tsp	salt	3 mL
1 cup	semisweet chocolate chips	250 mL

Preheat the oven to 400°F (200°C).

Cream the butter and sugar. Add the honey and eggs and beat well. Add the peanut butter and beat until well mixed. Stir in the milk and bran. Combine the flour, baking powder, baking soda and salt. Stir into the batter. Fold in the chocolate chips.

Fill greased muffin tins 3/4 full. Bake for 20 minutes.

Chocolate Cheesecake Muffins

Our grown-up version of a 'Twinkie' will be a hit with your friends and family.

PREPARATION TIME: 15 minutes
COOKING TIME: 20 minutes
YIELD: 12 muffins

3 oz	cream cheese	100 g
2 Tbsp	sugar	25 mL
3 Tbsp	cocoa	45 mL
1 cup	flour	250 mL
2 tsp	baking powder	10 mL
1/2 cup	sugar	125 mL
1/2 tsp	salt	2 mL
1	egg, beaten	1
3/4 cup	milk	175 mL
1/3 cup	oil	75 mL

Preheat the oven to 375°F (190°C).

Beat the cream cheese and sugar together in a small bowl. Set aside.

Combine the cocoa, flour, baking powder, sugar and salt in a large bowl. Make a well in the centre. Combine the egg, milk and oil and add all at once to the dry ingredients, stirring until just moistened.

Grease large muffin tins. Spoon 2 tablespoons (25 mL) of the chocolate batter into each cup. Drop 1 teaspoon (5 mL) of the cheese mixture on top and then add more chocolate batter.

Bake for 20 minutes.

Ginger Cheese Muffins

For a change from dessert-type muffins, try these with a salad for lunch. They are extraordinary.

PREPARATION TIME: 20 minutes
COOKING TIME: 20 minutes
YIELD: 12 large muffins

2 cups	flour	500 mL
3 tsp	baking powder	15 mL
1/4 tsp	baking soda	1 mL
1 tsp	ground ginger	5 mL
1/2 tsp	salt	2 mL
1	egg	1
1 cup	milk	250 mL
1/2 cup	corn syrup	125 mL
1/4 cup	shortening	50 mL
2/3 cup	grated cheese	150 mL
1 1/2 tsp	thinly sliced ginger root	7 mL

Preheat the oven to 350°F (180°C).

Sift together the flour, baking powder, baking soda, ground ginger and salt 3 times.

In a separate bowl, beat the egg until light. Add the milk and corn syrup.

Combine the two mixtures, stirring as little as possible. Add the shortening, cheese and ginger root and stir just to combine. Fill oiled muffin tins 2/3 full. Bake until firm. Cover and let stand 5 minutes before removing from the pan.

Oatmeal Muffins

If bran muffins bore you, perhaps oatmeal will give you a lift.

PREPARATION TIME: **15 minutes**
COOKING TIME: **25-30 minutes**
YIELD: **10 large muffins**

1 cup	old-fashioned rolled oats	250 mL
1 cup	milk	250 mL
1/2 cup	vegetable oil	125 mL
1/2 cup	packed brown sugar	125 mL
1	egg	1
1 cup	flour	250 mL
1/2 tsp	salt	2 mL
1/2 tsp	baking soda	2 mL
1 1/2 tsp	baking powder	7 mL

Preheat the oven to 350°F (180°C).

Combine the rolled oats, milk, oil, sugar and egg and mix thoroughly. Combine the remaining ingredients. Add to oatmeal mixture, stirring until just moistened.

Fill greased muffin tins 3/4 full. Bake 25 to 30 minutes, until brown.

Orange Muffins

Serve orange muffins with fruit-flavoured cream cheese at tea time.

PREPARATION TIME: 15 minutes
COOKING TIME: 18-20 minutes
YIELD: 12 muffins

2 cups	all-purpose flour	500 mL
1 Tbsp	baking powder	15 mL
1/2 tsp	salt	2 mL
1/4 cup	sugar	50 mL
	grated rind of 1 orange	
1/4 cup	orange juice	50 mL
1/4 cup	vegetable oil	50 mL
1	egg, lightly beaten	1
3/4 cup	milk	175 mL
1/2 cup	melted butter	125 mL
1-2 tsp	cinnamon	5-10 mL
1/4 cup	sugar	50 mL

Preheat the oven to 400°F (200°C).

Sift together the flour, baking powder, salt and sugar into a large bowl. Stir in the orange rind. Combine the orange juice, oil, egg and milk in a small bowl. Pour milk mixture into the dry ingredients. Stir quickly until just mixed but still lumpy. Quickly fill greased or paper-lined muffin tins 3/4 full. Bake for 18 to 20 minutes.

Brush tops with melted butter. Combine the cinnamon and sugar and sprinkle on top.

Zucchini Chocolate Muffins

The combination of zucchini and chocolate yields a moist, not too sweet muffin.

PREPARATION TIME: **20** minutes
COOKING TIME: **18** minutes
YIELD: **12 large muffins**

1/4 cup	soft margarine	50 mL
1/2 cup	vegetable oil	125 mL
1 cup	sugar	250 mL
2	eggs	2
2 cups	grated zucchini	500 mL
1/2 cup	sour milk	125 mL
2 cups	flour	500 mL
1/4 cup	cocoa	50 mL
1/2 Tbsp	baking powder	7.5 mL
1 tsp	baking soda	5 mL
1 tsp	cinnamon	5 mL
1 tsp	ground cloves	5 mL
1/4 cup	chocolate chips	50 mL

Preheat the oven to 350°F (180°C).

Combine the margarine, oil, sugar, eggs, zucchini and milk. In a separate bowl, combine the flour, cocoa, baking powder, baking soda, cinnamon and cloves. Add to the wet ingredients and stir briefly until just combined. Stir in the chocolate chips.

Spoon into greased muffin tins and bake for 18 minutes.

Apricot-Pecan Loaf

Pecans and apricots decorate each slice of this delicious loaf.

PREPARATION TIME: 15 minutes
COOKING TIME: 45 minutes
YIELD: 1 loaf

2 cups	bran flake cereal	500 mL
1/2 cup	all-purpose flour	125 mL
1/2 cup	whole wheat flour	125 mL
1/2 cup	sugar	125 mL
2 tsp	baking powder	10 mL
1/2 tsp	salt	2 mL
1/2 tsp	cinnamon	2 mL
1/2 cup	chopped dried apricots	125 mL
1/4 cup	finely chopped pecans	50 mL
1	egg, lightly beaten	1
1/2 cup	2% milk	125 mL
1/2 cup	orange juice	125 mL
1/4 cup	vegetable oil	50 mL

Preheat the oven to 350°F (180°C).

Crush the cereal to make 3/4 cup (175 mL) of crumbs. Stir together the flours, cereal, sugar, baking powder, salt, cinnamon, apricots and pecans.

Beat together the egg, milk, orange juice and oil. Add to the dry ingredients and beat for 1/2 minute. Turn into a greased 8-by-4 inch (1.5 L) loaf pan. Bake for 45 minutes or until a toothpick inserted in the centre comes out clean.

Cool 10 minutes before removing from the loaf pan. Allow to cool completely before slicing and wrapping. The loaf is best if wrapped in foil and allowed to sit overnight before slicing.

Lemon Bread

Unlike most lemon bread recipes, ours produces a loaf that is not cake-like in texture. Rather, it is dense and crumbly and full of the rich flavour of lemons and walnuts.

PREPARATION TIME: 5 minutes
COOKING TIME: 55 minutes
YIELD: 1 loaf

Loaf	6 Tbsp	butter	90 mL
	1 cup	sugar	250 mL
	2	eggs	2
	1 1/2 cups	flour	375 mL
	1/2 tsp	salt	2 mL
	1/2 cup	chopped walnuts	125 mL
		grated rind of 1 lemon	
Glaze	1/2 cup	sugar	125 mL
		juice of 1 lemon	

Preheat the oven to 325°F (160°C).

Loaf: Cream the butter with the sugar. Add the eggs, flour, salt, walnuts and lemon rind. The mixture will be very thick. Spoon into a 9-by-5 inch (2 L) loaf pan. Bake for 55 minutes.

Glaze: Combine the sugar and lemon juice. Pour over the hot bread after baking.

Beer Bread

Bread in less than an hour? Self-rising flour makes it possible; try different combinations of herbs and cheeses for individual variations.

PREPARATION TIME: 5 minutes
COOKING TIME: 55 minutes
YIELD: 1 loaf

1 bottle	beer	1 bottle
(12-oz)		(341 mL)
3 cups	self-rising flour	750 mL
1/4 cup	sugar	50 mL
1/4 cup	grated Swiss cheese	50 mL
1-2 Tbsp	chopped fresh dill	15-25 mL

Preheat the oven to 350°F (180°C).

Combine all the ingredients and pour into a greased 8-by-4 inch (1.5 L) loaf pan. Bake for 55 minutes.

Variation: Combine 1/4 cup (50 mL) grated Cheddar cheese with 1 to 2 tablespoons (15 to 25 mL) chopped chives.

DESSERTS

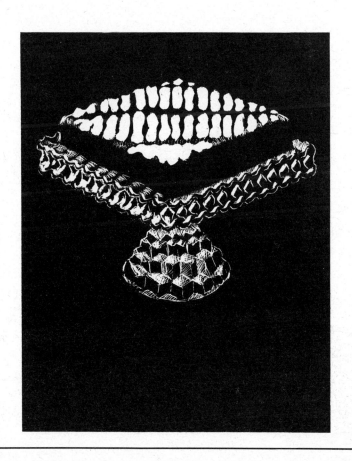

Almond Roca Ice Cream Torte

On a hot summer evening there is no better way to end the meal than with a frozen dessert. We've included five alternatives ranging from the simple to the spectacular.

Almond Roca Ice Cream Torte is an elegant dessert to serve at a summer buffet. While it takes a little extra effort to prepare, it is sure to earn rave reviews from your guests.

PREPARATION TIME: 45-50 minutes
REFRIGERATION TIME: 1 hour
YIELD: 10-12 servings

8 oz	semisweet chocolate	250 g
1 cup	35% cream	250 mL
1/2 tsp	instant coffee	2 mL
1 Tbsp	dark rum	15 mL
2-3 Tbsp	butter	25-45 mL
40	chocolate wafers	40
1 pt	dark chocolate ice cream	500 mL
1 pt	Swiss Mocha ice cream	500 mL
1 can (7-oz)	Almond Roca	1 can (200 g)
	chocolate shavings or chocolate coffee beans as garnish	

Combine the chocolate, cream, coffee and rum in a saucepan. Heat slowly until the chocolate is melted. Remove from the heat and cool.

While the chocolate is cooling melt the butter. Crush the wafers and mix with the butter. Use just enough butter so that the crumbs stick together lightly — they should not be wet. Press half of the crumbs into the bottom of a 9-inch (22 cm) springform pan.

Slightly soften ice creams. Spread the dark chocolate ice cream over the crumbs. Spoon on one-third of the sauce. It should have cooled enough so that it does not instantly melt the ice cream.

Press the rest of the crumbs over the sauce and top with another third of the sauce.

Spread on the mocha ice cream. Spoon on the remaining sauce.

Coarsely chop the Almond Roca. Sprinkle on top of the torte.

Cover the torte with plastic wrap and freeze until needed.

Before serving, if desired, garnish with chocolate shavings or chocolate coffee beans.

Lemon Frost

Treat your family to an instant gourmet dessert.

PREPARATION TIME: 15 minutes
FREEZING TIME: 2 hours
YIELD: 6 servings

1	egg, separated	1
1/3 cup	water	75 mL
1/3 cup	nonfat dry milk powder	75 mL
1/3 cup	sugar	75 mL
1/4 tsp	grated lemon rind	1 mL
2-3 Tbsp	lemon juice	25-45 mL
dash	salt	dash
1/4 cup	graham cracker crumbs	50 mL

Combine the egg white, water and dry milk and beat to stiff peaks.

Slightly beat the egg yolk and mix together with the sugar, lemon rind, lemon juice and salt. Fold into the egg white mixture.

Sprinkle 3 tablespoons (45 mL) cracker crumbs into a buttered 8-inch (2 L) square dish. Spoon in the lemon mixture. Dust with the remaining cracker crumbs. Freeze until firm, about 2 hours.

Freezer Lemon Pie

Prepare this attractive dessert the day before to allow the lemon to flavour the ice cream.

PREPARATION TIME: **20 minutes**
COOKING TIME: **15 minutes**
FREEZING TIME: **6-8 hours**
YIELD: **8 servings**

Filling

6 Tbsp	butter	90 mL
2	eggs, lightly beaten	2
2	egg yolks	2
1/3 cup	lemon juice	75 mL
	rind of 1 lemon, grated	
dash	salt	dash
1 cup	sugar	250 mL
1 qt	vanilla ice cream, partially softened	1 L
1 (9-in)	deep-dish pie crust, baked	1 (22 cm)

Meringue

3	egg whites	3
6 Tbsp	sugar	90 mL
1 tsp	cream of tartar	5 mL

Preheat the oven to 475°F (240°C).

Filling: Melt the butter in the top of a double boiler. Stir in the eggs and egg yolks. Add the lemon juice, lemon rind, salt and sugar. Cook over boiling water until thick. Cool. Layer the lemon sauce and ice cream in the pie crust, ending with sauce.

Meringue: Prepare the meringue by beating the egg whites until frothy and then gradually adding the sugar and the cream of tartar. Beat until stiff peaks form. Spread over the pie, covering the filling completely. Bake at 475°F (240°C) for 3 to 4 minutes. Freeze until set. This is best made the day ahead.

Remove the pie from the freezer 20 minutes before serving.

Lemon Cloud Sherbet

A light and refreshing dessert, Lemon Cloud Sherbet is an appropriate ending to a heavy meal.

PREPARATION TIME: **20 minutes**
FREEZING TIME: **2 hours**
YIELD: **6-8 servings**

3	eggs, separated	3
1/2 cup	sugar	125 mL
1/4 cup	fresh lemon juice	50 mL
dash	salt	dash
1 cup	35% cream	250 mL
2 tsp.	grated lemon rind	10 mL

Beat the egg yolks in a large bowl until thick. Gradually beat in the sugar. Add the lemon juice and salt. Separately beat the egg whites until thick, using clean beaters. Separately beat the cream until stiff. Gently fold the cream, egg whites and lemon rind into the yolk mixture. Put in an attractive serving bowl and freeze covered. Let soften in the refrigerator for 1/2 hour before serving.

The dessert is best served the same day. Excessive freezing will cause ice crystals to form.

Pastis Ice Cream with Bitter Chocolate Sauce

This wonderful concoction is rich and creamy. The anisette flavour will keep your guests guessing.

PREPARATION TIME: **20** minutes
COOKING TIME: **20** minutes
FREEZING TIME: **3** hours
YIELD: **6** servings ice cream; 1 1/2 cups (375 mL) sauce

Ice Cream

11 Tbsp	sugar	160 mL
5 Tbsp	water	75 mL
6	egg yolks	6
1 cup	35% cream	250 mL
1 1/2 Tbsp	anisette or Pernod	22 mL

Sauce

3 1/2 oz	unsweetened chocolate	100 g
3/4 cup	milk	175 mL
2 Tbsp	18% cream	25 mL
1 tsp	sugar	5 mL
1 1/2 Tbsp	butter	22 mL

Ice Cream: In a small, heavy saucepan boil 9 tablespoons (135 mL) of sugar in the water until the sugar has just dissolved. Turn down the heat. In the top of a double boiler, beat the egg yolks until thick. Return the syrup to a boil and slowly beat it into the yolks over hot water until the mixture is thick, foamy and coats a whisk. Remove from the hot water and continue to beat until cool.

Whip the cream with the remaining 2 tablespoons (25 mL) of sugar. Cool the egg yolk mixture to the same temperature as the cream. (The egg yolks can be stirred over a bowl of ice cubes.) Stir the anisette or Pernod into the custard, then fold in the cream.

Freeze in individual molds.

Sauce: Melt the chocolate. In a small, heavy saucepan heat the milk, cream and sugar until it starts to simmer. Blend in the chocolate and the butter. Remove from the heat and stir until cool.

To serve, pour a small amount of the sauce over each serving of ice cream. The sauce is quite bitter so adjust its quantity to your guests' tastes.

Amaretto Trifle

Your guests will think that you spent hours preparing this beautifully-presented and delicious trifle.

PREPARATION TIME: 15 minutes
SETTING TIME: 30 minutes
YIELD: 12 servings

1 large	raspberry-filled jelly roll	1 large
(12-oz)		(340 g)
1/2 cup	Amaretto	125 mL
2	bananas, sliced	2
1 can	fruit cocktail, drained	1 can
(19-oz)		(540 mL)
1 pkg	instant vanilla pudding	1 pkg
(3 1/2-oz)		(98 g)
2 cups	milk	500 mL
1/2 cup	35% cream	125 mL
1/2 cup	sliced almonds, toasted	125 mL

Slice jelly roll in 1/2-inch (1 cm) slices. Line a large, preferably straight-sided, glass bowl with the jelly roll slices, covering the bottom and sides completely. Sprinkle the Amaretto over the jelly roll. Arrange the banana slices over the bottom layer and top with the fruit cocktail.

Combine the pudding mix and milk according to the package instructions. Pour the pudding over the fruit. Refrigerate trifle for 1/2 hour or until set.

Just prior to serving, whip the cream and spread over the trifle. Sprinkle with toasted almonds.

Apple Almond Torte

Be an efficient epicure with our torte: it's simpler to make than it looks—
and it's scrumptious!

PREPARATION TIME: **25 minutes**
COOKING TIME: **35 minutes**
YIELD: **8-10 servings**

Bottom Layer

1/2 cup	butter, room temperature	125 mL
1/3 cup	sugar	75 mL
1/4 tsp	vanilla	1 mL
1 cup	flour	250 mL

Filling

8 oz	cream cheese, room temperature	250 g
1/4 cup	sugar	50 mL
1	egg	1
1/2 tsp	vanilla	2 mL

Top Layer

1/3 cup	sugar	75 mL
1/2 tsp	cinnamon	2 mL
4 cups	peeled and sliced apples	1 L
1/4 cup	sliced almonds	50 mL
	icing sugar, for topping	

Preheat the oven to 450°F (230°C).

Bottom Layer: Cream the butter, sugar and vanilla. Stir in the flour. Press
into the bottom and sides of a buttered 9-inch (22 cm) springform pan.

Filling: Beat the cream cheese and sugar together. Add the egg and vanilla.
Pour into the pastry-lined pan.

Top Layer: Combine the sugar and cinnamon in a large bowl. Toss the apples
in the mixture. Arrange the apples over the filling and sprinkle the almonds
on top.

Bake at 450°F (230°C) for 10 minutes. Reduce the heat to 400°F (200°C) and continue baking for a further 25 minutes.

The torte may be served warm or cold, dusted with a little icing sugar.

Lemon Cheesecake

Tart, smooth and surprisingly light, Lemon Cheesecake will become one of your favourites.

PREPARATION TIME: 10 minutes
COOKING TIME: 30-40 minutes
YIELD: 1 pie

Crust

1 1/4 cups	graham cracker crumbs	300 mL
1/3 cup	brown sugar	75 mL
1/3 cup	butter, melted	75 mL

Filling

1 pkg (8-oz)	cream cheese	1 pkg (250 g)
2 tsp	butter	10 mL
1/2 cup	sugar	125 mL
1	egg	1
2 tsp	flour	10 mL
2/3 cup	milk	150 mL
1/4 cup	lemon juice	50 mL
2 tsp	grated lemon rind	10 mL

Preheat the oven to 350°F (180°C).

Crust: Combine the crumbs, brown sugar and butter. Press into the bottom and sides of a 9-inch (22 cm) pie plate, reserving 2 tablespoons (25 mL) for the topping.

Filling: Beat together the cream cheese, butter, sugar and egg. Add the flour and milk. Stir in the lemon juice and rind. Pour into the pie plate. Top with the remaining crumbs. Bake for 30 to 40 minutes.

Sour Cream Cheesecake

There are many excellent cheesecake recipes. However, as a superb basic version, this one simply 'takes the cake'.

PREPARATION TIME: **30 minutes**
COOKING TIME: **25 minutes**
REFRIGERATION TIME: **overnight (8 hours)**
YIELD: **10 servings**

Crust

1 1/2 cups	graham cracker crumbs	375 mL
6 Tbsp	butter, melted	90 mL
1/4 cup	sugar	50 mL

Filling

3 pkg (8-oz)	cream cheese	3 pkg (250 g)
1/2 cup	sugar	125 mL
2	eggs	2

Topping

1/2 pt	sour cream	250 mL
3 Tbsp	sugar	45 mL
1 tsp	vanilla	5 mL

Preheat the oven to 350°F (180°C).

Crust: Combine the graham cracker crumbs, butter and sugar. Press into the bottom of a 10-inch (24 cm) springform pan. Bake for 10 minutes.

Filling: Beat the cream cheese, sugar and eggs until smooth. Pour into the pan and bake for 20 minutes. Remove from the oven and cool for 15 minutes.

Topping: Combine the sour cream, sugar and vanilla. Spread over the baked cheesecake. Return to the oven and bake for 5 more minutes.

Remove from the oven and cool to room temperature. Refrigerate overnight.

This cake can be decorated with slices of fresh strawberries and kiwi fruit.

Chilled Chocolate Loaf

Velvety and very rich, this chocolate loaf should be served in small portions.

PREPARATION TIME: **20** minutes
REFRIGERATION TIME: **4** hours
YIELD: **10** servings

8 oz	semisweet chocolate chips	250 g
1/4 cup	Grand Marnier or other liqueur	50 mL
8 oz	unsalted butter	250 g
2 Tbsp	sugar	25 mL
2	eggs, separated	2
1 1/2 cups	slivered almonds	375 mL
pinch	salt	pinch
	almonds as garnish (optional)	
	mandarin orange sections as garnish (optional)	

Grease an 8-by-4 inch (1.5 L) loaf pan with oil. Invert the pan on paper towels to drain excess oil.

In a heavy saucepan, melt the chocolate chips over low heat, stirring constantly. When melted, stir in the liqueur. Remove from the heat and cool to room temperature.

Cream the butter until fluffy. Beat in the sugar and the egg yolks, one at a time. Stir in the almonds and chocolate.

In a separate bowl, beat the egg whites and the salt until stiff peaks form. Fold into the chocolate mixture. Pour into the loaf pan, cover with plastic wrap and refrigerate for 4 hours.

Remove from the refrigerator 1 hour prior to serving. Run a knife around the sides of the pan and dip the bottom of the pan in hot water for a few seconds. Place a chilled serving dish over the pan and invert. Smooth the loaf. Garnish with almonds and mandarin orange slices if desired. Refrigerate until just prior to serving.

Chocolate Lime Swirl

The combination of a sweet chocolate crust and a tart lemony filling makes this dessert irresistible.

PREPARATION TIME: 45 minutes
REFRIGERATION TIME: 4 hours
YIELD: 10 servings

1/4 cup	butter	50 mL
1 1/2 pkg (7-oz)	chocolate wafers	1 1/2 pkg (200 g)
1 pkg (3-oz)	lime jelly powder	1 pkg (85 g)
1/2 cup	boiling water	125 mL
1/3 cup	lemon juice	75 mL
1/4 cup	sugar	50 mL
1 can (13 1/2-oz)	evaporated milk, chilled in refrigerator for at least 3 days	1 can (385 mL)
3 drops	green food colouring	3 drops

Put the mixing beaters and bowl in the refrigerator and chill for 15 to 20 minutes.

Melt the butter and pour into a bowl.

Set aside 14 chocolate wafers. Crush the remaining wafers and mix with the melted butter. Pat the crumbs into the bottom of a greased 9-inch (22 cm) springform pan. Save some of the crumb mixture for garnish. Place the whole cookies on edge around the side of the pan. Refrigerate.

Dissolve the jelly powder in the boiling water. Add the lemon juice and the sugar. If necessary, add more lemon juice—the mixture should be quite tart.

Whip the evaporated milk until stiff, about 3 to 4 minutes. Add the jelly powder mixture to the milk and continue beating until well blended. Stir in the food colouring and pour into the springform pan. Sprinkle the remaining chocolate wafer crumbs on top.

Chill for at least 4 hours prior to serving.

Chocolate Mousse

Of the countless recipes for chocolate mousse, ours is truly 'la crème de la crème'.

PREPARATION TIME: **20 minutes**
REFRIGERATION TIME: **3-4 hours**
YIELD: **8 servings**

1 pkg (12-oz)	semisweet chocolate chips	1 pkg (350 g)
1/2 cup	strong coffee	125 mL
2	eggs, separated	2
2-4 Tbsp	any liqueur	25-50 mL
pinch	cream of tartar	pinch
2 Tbsp	sugar	25 mL
1 cup	35% cream	250 mL

Set the chocolate chips and the coffee in the top of a double boiler over boiling water. Stir until the chocolate is melted. Remove from the heat and stir in the egg yolks and liqueur.

Beat the egg whites with the cream of tartar until almost stiff. Gradually add the sugar and beat until stiff peaks form. Fold the egg whites into the chocolate. Whip the cream and fold into the mousse. Chill for 3 to 4 hours.

Chocolate Torte

Flour is not required to make this fabulous cake-like dessert.

PREPARATION TIME: **15** minutes plus **10** minutes after baking
COOKING TIME: **20** minutes
YIELD: **8** servings

1/2 cup	salted butter	125 mL
1 1/2 cups	icing sugar	375 mL
4	eggs, separated	4
4 oz	unsweetened chocolate, melted	112 g
1 cup	chopped nuts icing sugar as garnish	250 mL

Preheat the oven to 350°F (180°C).

Grease two 9-inch (1.5 L) round pans.

Cream the butter and icing sugar. Add the egg yolks. Stir in the melted chocolate and nuts.

In a separate bowl, beat the egg whites until stiff. Fold into the chocolate mixture.

Separate the mixture into thirds. Pour one-third into one pan, one-third into the second pan and reserve the last third.

Bake the two pans in the oven for 20 minutes. Remove to a wire rack to cool. Turn cakes out of pans. Place one layer on a serving dish. Spread the reserved mixture on top then place the second layer on top. Sprinkle with icing sugar. Refrigerate until serving.

Hazelnut Torte

Your guests will rave about your baking expertise when you present this dessert. Only you will know how easy it was to make.

PREPARATION TIME: **20-25** minutes
COOKING TIME: **20** minutes
YIELD: **8-10** servings

Cake

1 cup	hazelnuts, with skins	250 mL
4	eggs	4
3/4 cup	sugar	175 mL
2 Tbsp	flour	25 mL

Filling

1/3 cup	butter, softened	75 mL
2 cups	icing sugar	500 mL
1-2 Tbsp	hot strong coffee	15-25 mL
1 tsp	cocoa	5 mL
1 tsp	vanilla	5 mL

Topping

1 cup	35% cream	250 mL
1 Tbsp	chocolate or coffee liqueur	15 mL
	chocolate shavings as garnish	
	chocolate covered coffee beans as garnish	

Preheat the oven to 350°F (180°C).

Cake: Bake the hazelnuts for 5 to 10 minutes. Blend all the cake ingredients in a blender. Pour the batter into 2 greased 8-inch (1.3 L) round layer pans. Bake for 20 minutes. Cool.

Filling: Combine all the ingredients. Spread between the cake layers and on the top and sides.

Topping: Whip the cream with the liqueur. Spread on top of the cake. Garnish with the grated chocolate and coffee beans.

Apple Spice Cake

Wholesome, healthy and delicious, Apple Spice Cake can be served for breakfast or dessert.

PREPARATION: **25** minutes
COOKING TIME: **35** minutes
YIELD: **12** servings

1/2 cup	unsalted butter or margarine, room temperature	125 mL
1 cup	honey	250 mL
1 tsp	brown sugar	5 mL
1	egg	1
1 tsp	vanilla	5 mL
1 cup	whole wheat flour	250 mL
1 1/4 cups	all-purpose flour	300 mL
1 tsp	baking soda	5 mL
1/2 tsp	salt	2 mL
1 tsp	cinnamon	5 mL
1/2 tsp	nutmeg	2 mL
1/4 tsp	cloves	1 mL
1/4 tsp	allspice or ginger	1 mL
1/2 cup	chopped nuts	125 mL
1/4 cup	chopped dates	50 mL
1 cup	applesauce	250 mL

Preheat the oven to 325°F (160°C).

Cream the butter in a large bowl. Gradually add the honey, beating until light and fluffy. Add the brown sugar, egg and vanilla. Mix well.

In a medium bowl, stir together the flour, baking soda, salt and spices. Coat the nuts and dates with approximately 2 tablespoons (25 mL) of the flour mixture and set aside.

Add the flour mixture to the creamed mixture alternately with the applesauce, beginning and ending with the flour. Stir in the nuts and the dates.

Grease the bottom of a 9-by-13 inch (4 L) pan. Pour in the batter. Bake for 35 minutes, or until cake tests done.

Cool and cut into squares. These squares are delicious served with dollops of whipped cream.

Blueberry Cake

A down-East treat, Jane's blueberry cake is sure to become a favourite across the country.

PREPARATION TIME: 20 minutes
COOKING TIME: 30 minutes
YIELD: 8 servings

2 cups	all-purpose flour	500 mL
3 tsp	baking powder	15 mL
1/2 tsp	salt	2 mL
1 cup	sugar	250 mL
1/2 cup	shortening	125 mL
1 cup	blueberries, fresh or frozen	250 mL
1 cup	milk	250 mL
2	eggs, well beaten	2

Preheat the oven to 375°F (190°C).

Sift together the flour, baking powder, salt and sugar. Cut in the shortening. Mix in the berries. Combine the milk and the beaten eggs. Stir into the dry ingredients.

Pour batter into a buttered 8-inch (2 L) square cake pan.

Bake for approximately 30 minutes. The top of the cake will become quite brown.

If desired, serve with whipped cream or vanilla ice cream.

Sylvia's Peach Kuchen

Delicious hot or cold, our peach cake is also a time-saver.

PREPARATION TIME: 15 minutes
COOKING TIME: 45 minutes
YIELD: 6-8 servings

Base

2 cups	flour	500 mL
1/2 tsp	baking powder	2 mL
pinch	salt	pinch
3 Tbsp	sugar	45 mL
3/4 cup	butter	175 mL

Filling

8	peaches, peeled and sliced	8
1 tsp	cinnamon	5 mL
1/4 cup	sugar	50 mL

Topping

2	egg yolks	2
1 cup	sour cream	250 mL
1 Tbsp	sugar	15 mL

Preheat the oven to 400°F (200°C).

Base: Mix together the flour, baking powder, salt and sugar. Cut in the butter until the mixture is crumbly. Press into the bottom of a 9-by-13 inch (4 L) baking dish.

Filling: Arrange the peach slices on top of the base. Sprinkle with the cinnamon and sugar. Bake for 15 minutes.

Topping: Beat together the egg yolks and sour cream. Stir in the remaining sugar. Pour on top of peach slices. Turn the oven down to 350°F (180°C) and continue baking for 30 minutes.

Serve hot or cold.

Brandied Pineapple Cake

Because this recipe yields a large quantity for a small amount of effort, it is ideal to bring to a potluck dinner.

PREPARATION TIME: 15 minutes
COOKING TIME: 45 minutes
YIELD: 18-25 pieces

Cake

2	eggs	2
1 1/2 cups	sugar	375 mL
2 tsp	baking soda	10 mL
1/2 tsp	salt	2 mL
1 can	crushed pineapple	1 can
(14-oz)		(398 mL)
2 cups	flour	500 mL

Icing

3/4 cup	sugar	175 mL
1/2 cup	milk	125 mL
1/2 cup	butter	125 mL
1 tsp	brandy	5 mL

Preheat the oven to 350°F (180°C).

Cake: Beat the eggs lightly. Stir in the sugar, baking soda, salt and pineapple. Add the flour. Pour into a greased 9-by-13 inch (4 L) baking pan. Bake for 45 minutes.

Icing: Prepare while the cake is baking. Boil together the sugar, milk and butter. Remove from the heat and stir in the brandy. Spread the icing over the hot cake. (This recipe makes a lot of icing but use it all.)

Serve warm with whipped cream or vanilla ice cream.

The cake will keep for several days in the refrigerator. It also freezes well.

Chocolate Chip Brownies

Simple to whip up, these addictive beauties are moist and flavourful. They are rich with chocolate and not overly sweet.

PREPARATION TIME: **15 minutes**
COOKING TIME: **20-25 minutes**
YIELD: **16 squares**

1/3 cup	butter or margarine	75 mL
2 oz	bitter chocolate	56 g
1 cup	dark brown sugar	250 mL
2	eggs, beaten	2
1/4 cup	flour	50 mL
1/4 tsp	baking powder	1 mL
1/4 tsp	cinnamon	1 mL
1 tsp	vanilla	5 mL
1/4 cup	chocolate chips	50 mL
1/4 cup	pecan or walnut pieces (optional)	50 mL

Preheat the oven to 350°F (180°C).

Melt the butter or margarine and chocolate in a double boiler. Remove from the heat and stir in the sugar, eggs, flour, baking powder, cinnamon and vanilla. Mix well. Add the chocolate chips and nuts. Pour into a well-greased 8-inch (2 L) square pan. Bake for 20 to 25 minutes.

Allow to cool slightly, then cut into squares.

These are very good served warm from the oven with ice cream on the side.

Kahlua Brownies

These are extremely rich with a real kick! Be sure to double the recipe as they will disappear in no time.

PREPARATION TIME: 15 minutes
COOKING TIME: 25-30 minutes
YIELD: 40 squares

Brownies

1 cup	butter	250 mL
1 cup	white sugar	250 mL
1 cup	packed brown sugar	250 mL
3/4 cup	cocoa	175 mL
3 large	eggs	3 large
1 cup	flour	250 mL
1 1/2 tsp	baking powder	7 mL
1 1/2 tsp	vanilla	7 mL
1 Tbsp	Kahlua	15 mL

Icing

1/2 cup	butter, softened	125 mL
1 cup	icing sugar	250 mL
2/3 cup	cocoa	150 mL
1 tsp	vanilla	5 mL
1 Tbsp	milk	15 mL
2 Tbsp	Kahlua	25 mL
2 Tbsp	hot coffee	25 mL

Preheat the oven to 350°F (180°C).

Brownies: Melt the butter and combine with the sugars and cocoa in a large bowl. Beat in the eggs one at a time. Sift the flour and baking powder into the mixture and stir. Add the vanilla and Kahlua.

Pour into a greased and floured 9-by-13 inch (4 L) cake pan. Bake for 25 to 30 minutes. The centre should be soft. Let cool before icing.

Icing: Combine ingredients with an electric mixer. Spread over the brownies.

Chocolate Mint Squares

The secret to these luscious squares is the bitter glaze that cuts the sweetness—a chocaholic's dream!

PREPARATION TIME: 30 minutes
COOKING TIME: 20-25 minutes
YIELD: 16 squares

Squares

2 oz	unsweetened chocolate	56 g
1/2 cup	butter	125 mL
2	eggs	2
1 cup	sugar	250 mL
1/4 tsp	peppermint flavouring	1 mL
1/2 cup	flour	125 mL
pinch	salt	pinch

Icing

1 cup	icing sugar	250 mL
2 Tbsp	butter, room temperature	25 mL
1 Tbsp	10% cream or milk	15 mL
3/4 tsp	peppermint flavouring	3 mL

Glaze

1 oz	unsweetened chocolate	28 g
1 Tbsp	butter	15 mL

Preheat the oven to 350°F (180°C).

Squares: Melt the chocolate and butter together. Cool slightly. Beat the eggs until frothy and stir in the sugar, chocolate and peppermint. Add the flour and salt. Turn into a greased 9-inch (2.5 L) square pan. Bake for 20 to 25 minutes.

Icing: Work the butter into the icing sugar. Add the cream and the peppermint. Blend until creamy. Spread on top of the cake after it has cooled slightly. Place the cake in the refrigerator while preparing the glaze.

Glaze: Melt the chocolate and butter, stirring until smooth. Drizzle the glaze over the cool, firm icing. Tilt back and forth until the surface is covered. Refrigerate at least 5 minutes.

Cut into squares. Serve the squares alone or with ice cream.

Crispy Fudge

We suggest you add some crunch to your fudge. Children and adults alike will enjoy it.

PREPARATION TIME: 15 minutes
REFRIGERATION TIME: 2 hours
YIELD: 48 squares

2 cups	semisweet chocolate chips	500 mL
1/2 cup	butter	125 mL
1/2 cup	corn syrup	125 mL
2 tsp	vanilla	10 mL
1 cup	icing sugar, sifted	250 mL
4 cups	crisp rice cereal	1 L

Melt together the chocolate chips, butter and corn syrup over low heat. Remove from the heat. Add the vanilla.

Stir in the icing sugar until smooth. Add the cereal and mix until thoroughly combined.

Spread into a lightly greased 9-by-13 inch (4 L) pan. Chill until set. Cut into 1 1/2-inch (3.75 cm) squares.

Super-Select Date Squares

We tested four date square recipes in order to choose the best date square ever. This recipe now combines the top-rated filling with the number one topping.

PREPARATION TIME: 15 minutes
COOKING TIME: 35-40 minutes
YIELD: 20-30 squares

Filling

1 lb	dates, pitted and chopped	500 g
1 1/2 cups	water	375 mL
1/2 tsp	lemon juice	2 mL
1 Tbsp	butter	15 mL
1/2 tsp	vanilla	2 mL

Topping

1 cup	sifted flour	250 mL
dash	salt	dash
1/2 tsp	baking soda	2 mL
1 cup	unsalted butter	250 mL
1 cup	packed brown sugar	250 mL
2 cups	old-fashioned rolled oats	500 mL

Preheat the oven to 325°F (160°C).

Filling: Combine the dates, water and lemon juice in a saucepan. Boil until creamy soft, adding more water if necessary. Stir in the butter and vanilla. Remove from the heat.

Topping: Sift together the flour, salt and baking soda. Cut in the butter. Add the sugar and the rolled oats. Mix well with a pastry blender.

Spread one-half of the mixture on the bottom of a buttered 8-inch (2 L) square pan. Pat to make the surface smooth. Spread the date mixture on top. Cover with the remaining topping and smooth out the surface.

Bake for 35 to 40 minutes, or until golden brown. Try serving these date squares hot, topped with vanilla ice cream.

Maple Walnut Squares

A delightful variation on chocolate brownies, 'beigies' will be a welcome addition to your dessert repertoire.

PREPARATION TIME: 15 minutes
COOKING TIME: 25 minutes
YIELD: 25 squares

Squares

2/3 cup	sifted all-purpose flour	150 mL
dash	salt	dash
1/2 tsp	baking powder	2 mL
3/4 cup	chopped walnuts	175 mL
1/4 cup	butter, room temperature	50 mL
1/2 cup	white sugar	125 mL
1/2 cup	brown sugar	125 mL
2	eggs, lightly beaten	2
1 tsp	vanilla	5 mL

Icing

1 1/4 cups	icing sugar	300 mL
1/4 cup	butter, room temperature	50 mL
3 Tbsp	milk	45 mL
1 tsp	maple flavouring	5 mL

Preheat the oven to 350°F (180°C).

Squares: Combine the flour, salt, baking powder and walnuts in a small bowl. In a medium bowl, cream together the butter and the sugars. Add the eggs and vanilla. Stir the flour mixture into the wet ingredients until well mixed. Pour batter into a buttered 8-inch (2 L) square baking dish. Bake for 25 minutes. Cool.

Icing: Combine the icing ingredients until smooth. Spread on squares. Cut and serve.

Liqueur Pie

Try this refreshing dessert on a hot summer afternoon for a boozy treat.

PREPARATION TIME: 45 minutes
COOKING TIME: 15 minutes
REFRIGERATION TIME: several hours or overnight
YIELD: 10 servings

Crust

1 pkg (8-oz)	chocolate wafers, crumbled	1 pkg (250 g)
1/4 cup	butter	50 mL

Filling

1/2 cup	water	125 mL
1 envelope (1-Tbsp)	unflavoured gelatin	1 envelope (7 g)
2/3 cup	sugar	150 mL
3	eggs, separated	3
1/2 cup	Grand Marnier	125 mL
	grated rind of 1 orange	
1 cup	35% cream, whipped	250 mL

Preheat the oven to 350°F (180°C).

Crust: Set aside 1/4 cup (50 mL) of the chocolate wafer crumbs. Melt the butter. Combine the remaining crumbs and the butter. Pat into the bottom of a 9-inch (22 cm) springform pan. Bake for 15 minutes, or until slightly crisp.

Filling: Pour the water into a saucepan and sprinkle the gelatin on top. Stir to dissolve while heating gently. Add half the sugar and the egg yolks. Cook until mixture is thick, stirring constantly. Do not boil. Remove from the heat.

Transfer the gelatin mixture to a large bowl. Stir in the Grand Marnier and the orange rind. Chill until the mixture mounds slightly (about 10 minutes).

Beat the egg whites until stiff. Add the remaining sugar and continue beating until stiff peaks form.

Gently fold the egg whites into the Grand Marnier mixture. Fold in the whipped cream. Pour the mixture over the crust and top with the remaining chocolate wafer crumbs. Chill several hours or overnight before serving.

Variation: Substitute crème de menthe for the Grand Marnier and omit the orange rind.

Mocha Truffles

These delightful morsels taste great straight from the freezer. They can be served in small baking cups.

PREPARATION TIME: **50 minutes**
REFRIGERATION TIME: **1-2 hours**
YIELD: **4 dozen**

1 pkg (6-oz)	semisweet chocolate chips	1 pkg (175 g)
2/3 cup	butter, room temperature	150 mL
1	egg yolk	1
1 1/4 cups	icing sugar	300 mL
1 Tbsp	rum	15 mL
1 tsp	instant coffee	5 mL
1 cup	chocolate wafer crumbs	250 mL

Melt the chocolate chips over hot water. Cool. Cream the butter. Blend in the egg yolk and the sugar. Add the chocolate, rum and instant coffee. Mix well. Chill 1 to 2 hours until the mixture is firm enough to handle.

Drop the mixture by teaspoonfuls into the crumbs. Cover with the crumbs and form into balls. Chill several hours. Store in a tightly covered container.

Peanut Butter Balls

Freezing these treats will not stop your family from eating them. They taste even better frozen!

PREPARATION TIME: **20** minutes
REFRIGERATION TIME: **1** hour
YIELD: **30** balls

1 cup	crisp rice cereal	250 mL
1 cup	peanut butter	250 mL
1 cup	icing sugar	250 mL
1/4 cup	butter	50 mL
1/2 cup	dessicated coconut	125 mL
6 oz	semisweet chocolate chips	175 g

Combine the cereal, peanut butter, icing sugar, butter and coconut. Refrigerate for 1 hour.

Remove from refrigerator and roll the mixture into walnut-sized balls.

Melt the chocolate chips in the top of a double boiler. Dip the balls in the chocolate mixture. Place on a cookie sheet covered with wax paper and chill until serving time.

Chocolate Chip Raisin Cookies

These chewy cookies will please friends and family of all ages.

PREPARATION TIME: **10** minutes
COOKING TIME: **8-10** minutes
YIELD: **75** cookies

1 cup	butter, softened	250 mL
1 cup	packed brown sugar	250 mL
3/4 cup	white sugar	175 mL
2	eggs	2
1 tsp	vanilla	5 mL
2 cups	flour	500 mL
1 tsp	baking soda	5 mL
1 tsp	salt	5 mL
2 cups	semisweet chocolate chips	500 mL
1 cup	raisins	250 mL

Preheat the oven to 350°F (180°C).

Cream the butter and sugars until light and fluffy. Add the eggs and vanilla and mix well.

Sift together the flour, baking soda and salt. Stir into the batter and mix thoroughly. Add chocolate chips and raisins.

Drop the dough by teaspoonfuls onto greased cookie sheets.

Bake for 8 to 10 minutes. The centres should still be soft when the cookies are removed from the oven. Cool on the sheet for 5 minutes, then transfer to a wire rack.

Comfort Cookies

We've called them Comfort Cookies because they're big, thick and chewy and remind us of the cookies our mothers used to make. Try them with applesauce or ice cream.

PREPARATION TIME: **15 minutes**
COOKING TIME: **15 minutes**
YIELD: **2 dozen large cookies**

1 cup	butter, room temperature	250 mL
1 1/2 cups	packed brown sugar	375 mL
3 Tbsp	honey	45 mL
2	eggs	2
1 1/2 cups	all-purpose flour	375 mL
1 1/2 tsp	cinnamon	7 mL
1 tsp	cloves	5 mL
1/2 tsp	nutmeg	2 mL
1 tsp	salt	5 mL
4 cups	old-fashioned rolled oats	1 L
3/4 cup	raisins	175 mL
3/4 cup	chopped dates	175 mL

Preheat the oven to 375°F (190°C).

Lightly butter cookie sheets.

Cream the butter and sugar. Beat in the honey and eggs until the mixture is smooth. Sift together the flour, cinnamon, cloves, nutmeg and salt. Stir into the butter mixture, using a wooden spoon. Add the rolled oats, raisins and dates. Stir until well mixed.

Take the dough by tablespoons and shape into balls. Place on a cookie sheet 2 inches (5 cm) apart. Flatten the balls with the palm of your hand. (You may need to run cold water on your hands from time to time.)

Bake until the cookies are lightly browned.

Remove to a wire rack to cool.

Gingersnaps

A nice change from chocolate chip cookies, these gingersnaps are great for an after-school snack.

PREPARATION TIME: 35 minutes
COOKING TIME: 8-10 minutes
YIELD: 40 cookies

2 cups	flour	500 mL
1 tsp	ginger	5 mL
2 tsp	baking soda	10 mL
3/4 cup	shortening	175 mL
1 cup	sugar	250 mL
1	egg	1
1/4 cup	molasses	50 mL
	sugar for rolling	

Preheat the oven to 350°F (180°C).

Combine the flour, ginger and baking soda and set aside.

Cream the shortening, adding the sugar gradually. Beat in the egg and molasses. Add 1/4 cup (50 mL) of dry ingredients and mix well. Continue adding the dry ingredients until well blended.

Form teaspoonfuls of dough in the palm of your hand. Roll in sugar. Place 2 inches (5 cm) apart on an ungreased cookie sheet.

Bake for 8 to 10 minutes.

Potato Chip Cookies

These taste just like rich shortbread cookies. No one will guess that your secret ingredient is potato chips, and no one can eat just one.

PREPARATION TIME: **20 minutes**
COOKING TIME: **15 minutes**
YIELD: **3 dozen cookies**

1 cup	butter or margarine, room temperature	250 mL
1/2 cup	white sugar	125 mL
1/2 cup	crushed potato chips	125 mL
1/2 cup	chopped walnuts or pecans	125 mL
2 cups	flour	500 mL
	sugar for dipping	

Preheat the oven to 350°F (180°C).

Cream the butter and sugar until very soft. Add the potato chips, nuts and flour.

Form the dough into balls, place on greased cookie sheets and press flat with a fork dipped in sugar. Bake for 15 minutes.

Wedding Cookies

For any festive occasion, from afternoon tea to weddings, serve these melt-in-your-mouth cookies.

PREPARATION TIME: **20 minutes**
COOKING TIME: **20 minutes**
YIELD: **36 cookies**

1 cup	salted butter	250 mL
1/2 cup	icing sugar	125 mL
1 tsp	vanilla	5 mL
1 Tbsp	water	15 mL
2 cups	flour	500 mL
1 cup	chopped walnuts	250 mL

Preheat the oven to 300°F (150°C).

Cream the butter and half the sugar. Add the vanilla and the water. Stir in the flour. Add the walnuts.

Form the dough into tiny crescents, 1 1/2 inches (3.75 cm) long. Place on ungreased cookie sheets. Bake for 20 minutes or until the underside is brown.

Sprinkle the cookies with remaining icing sugar while they are still hot, and again when they have cooled.

Eleanor's Oranges

We do not know Eleanor, but we certainly enjoyed this refreshing, light dessert.

PREPARATION TIME: **10 minutes**
YIELD: **6 servings**

6	navel oranges	6
1/2 cup	sugar	125 mL
1/4 cup	liqueur: Curaçao, brandy or	50 mL
	Grand Marnier	

Peel and thinly slice the oranges. Put in a heatproof baking dish. Caramelize the sugar by heating it in a saucepan until the sugar turns brown. Pour the sugar over the oranges. The caramel will harden immediately. Sprinkle the liqueur or brandy over the caramelized oranges.

Cover with plastic wrap and leave on the counter overnight. Do not refrigerate. If you prefer an ice cold dessert, refrigerate the oranges when dinner is served.

Strawberry Dips

Try these delicious mouthfuls on a picnic or boat outing. Strawberries have never tasted so yummy!

PREPARATION TIME: **20 minutes**
YIELD: **4 servings**

1 pt	35% cream	500 mL
1 pt	sour cream	500 mL
1/4 cup	brown sugar	50 mL
2 Tbsp	dark rum	25 mL
2 Tbsp	Grand Marnier or brandy	25 mL
1 qt	strawberries	1 L

Beat the cream until stiff. Combine the sour cream, sugar and liquors. Fold into the whipped cream.

Dip the strawberries into the cream mixture and pop into your mouth.

At a large table, use fondue forks for a novel serving method.

Pineapple Plus

This simple-to-prepare and attractive dessert complements a time-consuming main course.

PREPARATION TIME: **10** minutes
YIELD: **8** sandwiches

1 pkg (8-oz)	cream cheese, room temperature	1 pkg (250 g)
2 Tbsp	pineapple juice	25 mL
2 1/2 tsp	grated orange rind	12 mL
1 tsp	white sugar	5 mL
2 cans (19-oz)	pineapple slices, drained	2 cans (540 mL)
1 pkg (15-oz)	frozen strawberries, thawed	1 pkg (425 g)

Combine the cream cheese, juice, rind and sugar. Assemble each sandwich by spreading a portion of the cheese mixture on a slice of pineapple and topping with a second slice. Repeat until all the cheese mixture and pineapple slices are used. Spoon the strawberries on top.

Coffee Supreme

Your guests will appreciate the extravagance of this special coffee.

PREPARATION TIME: 15 minutes
YIELD: 4 servings

3 Tbsp	coffee liqueur	45 mL
2 Tbsp	crème de cacao	25 mL
1 Tbsp	brandy	15 mL
2 cups	strong hot coffee	500 mL
4 sticks	cinnamon	4 sticks
1/2 cup	35% cream, whipped	125 mL

Combine the coffee liqueur, crème de cacao and brandy in a saucepan. Pour in the coffee; heat through but do not bring to a boil. Pour the coffee into four coffee cups, adding the cinnamon sticks as stirrers. Top the coffee with dollops of whipped cream. Serve immediately.

The coffee can also be served in demitasse cups, which will yield 5 to 6 servings.

Grand Marnier Coffee

Grand Marnier and whipped cream combine with coffee to create a fabulous ending to a special dinner.

PREPARATION TIME: 15 minutes
YIELD: 4 servings

4 cups	hot coffee	1 L
3/4 cup	Grand Marnier	175 mL
5 Tbsp	35% cream, whipped	75 mL
	chocolate shavings as	
	garnish	

Pour hot coffee into serving cups. Add 3 Tbsp (45 mL) of Grand Marnier to each cup. Top with a dollop of whipped cream. Garnish with shavings of chocolate.

TIPS FOR LIVING

We have assembled a few tips to speed your way in the kitchen. Some you may know already; we hope that you will find new ideas to incorporate into your own techniques.

To start:
• When approaching a recipe read it through first and assemble all of your ingredients. The French call this 'mise en place'.

A few ideas for preparing specific ingredients:
• To peel a clove of garlic, smash it first with the side of a knife or cleaver; peel should then lift away easily.

• Keep onions in the refrigerator or place them briefly in the freezer for tearless chopping.

• Roll lemons on the counter or drop them into hot water for a few minutes before cutting or squeezing to make the juice flow.

• To coarsely crush spices such as allspice or peppercorns, use a sturdy garlic press.

• Chill whipping cream, bowls and beaters in the freezer for a few minutes before whipping.

• Beef will slice into thin strips easily if it is partly frozen; place it in the freezer for 30 to 45 minutes.

• Add parsley stems to the stock pot rather than leaves—the flavour is more concentrated and the stems are faster to prepare.

• Remove the pits from black olives by bruising olives slightly against the kitchen counter with the bottom of a heavy glass or mallet. Then ease the pits out with the thumb and forefinger.

To speed things along:
• Potatoes will bake more quickly if they have been impaled on aluminum skewers.

• Meat loaf will cook in about 15 minutes if individual containers are used, such as small foil pans or muffin tins.

• Boiling time is reduced if sugar or salt is dissolved in the water.

• Cooked or stewed mixtures which include tomatoes will cook more quickly if the tomatoes are added toward the end of the cooking time.

• Speed up greasing by using liquid salad oil and spreading with a paper towel. Use muffin papers in any recipe where greased muffin tins are required.

• For sticky cutting jobs, first spray the knife with non-stick vegetable spray.

• To chill a bottle of wine or champagne quickly, whirl it around in a bucket of ice water to which a couple of handfuls of coarse salt has been added.

• Precut butter into blocks of 2 tablespoons (25 mL) each, and rewrap in original wrapper (note: a pound of butter equals 32 tablespoons).

A few thoughts on using, storing and freezing leftovers:
• Thin leftover dip with milk and use as salad dressing.

• Additional herbs are needed when reheating leftovers as some of the flavour is lost in storage.

• To salvage old cheese, grate and freeze it in small packages for topping casseroles.

• To simplify cooking frozen foods, freeze leftovers in ziplock bags, placing the sealed bag inside the utensil it will be cooked in so food takes the desired shape. Chill unfrozen leftovers in the container in which it will be heated later.

• For easy, delicious chicken broth, make up a batch of your own favourite chicken soup in concentrated form (use half the water). Strain. Freeze the concentrate in ice cube trays, then place cubes in a plastic bag and store in the freezer. Later, when you need a cup of broth, simply dissolve one of the cubes in enough boiling water to make a cup.

• Other convenient freezables include zest (rind), bread crumbs and pesto— prepare in quantity and freeze.

Clean up time can also be shortened:
• Keep a plastic bag on the counter in which to put garbage as you go along.

A couple of food processor tips:
• When pouring a mixture from the work bowl to another container, keep the steel blade in place by inserting your middle finger in the blade's centre post from the bottom.

• To clean the work bowl after most of the mixture has been removed, simply replace bowl on the base, cover, and pulse 2 or 3 times to remove excess mixture from the blade. Remove the blade and use your scraper to remove the last of the mixture quickly and easily.

To use the microwave as an adjunct to conventional cooking, try the following:

• Use the microwave to:
- melt butter and chocolate
- heat brandy (in a glass) for flambés
- warm ingredients (e.g. stocks, milk)
- bring refrigerated butter to room temperature (carefully!!)
- partially bake potatoes and finish them off in the oven

• To prepare ingredients you may:
- use it to peel peaches or tomatoes (score the ends in an 'X' and heat for 15 seconds on high)
- clarify butter
- toast nuts and seeds
- dry fresh herbs

• To freshen stale ingredients:
- moisten bread
- soften lumpy brown sugar
- plump dried raisins
- liquify crystallized honey

Index

In Good Time

Please send me _____ copy/copies of IN GOOD TIME at $14.95 per copy plus $2.00 for postage and handling.   TOTAL $_____

☐ Cheque or money order payable to
   The Barbra Schlifer Commemorative Clinic

☐ Charge to Visa/Mastercard # _____
   Expiry Date   _____

NAME: _____

ADDRESS: _____

CITY/TOWN: _____ PROVINCE: _____ CODE: _____

SIGNATURE:_____

Mail to: The Barbra Schlifer Commemorative Clinic Cookbook
         98 Chiltern Hill Road
         Toronto, Ontario
         M6C 3C1

In Good Time

Please send me _____ copy/copies of IN GOOD TIME at $14.95 per copy plus $2.00 for postage and handling.   TOTAL $_____

☐ Cheque or money order payable to
   The Barbra Schlifer Commemorative Clinic

☐ Charge to Visa/Mastercard # _____
   Expiry Date   _____

NAME: _____

ADDRESS: _____

CITY/TOWN: _____ PROVINCE: _____ CODE: _____

SIGNATURE:_____

Mail to: The Barbra Schlifer Commemorative Clinic Cookbook
         98 Chiltern Hill Road
         Toronto, Ontario
         M6C 3C1

In Good Time

Please send me _____ copy/copies of IN GOOD TIME at $14.95 per copy plus
$2.00 for postage and handling. TOTAL $_____

    ☐ Cheque or money order payable to
       The Barbra Schlifer Commemorative Clinic

    ☐ Charge to Visa/Mastercard # _____
       Expiry Date   _____

NAME: _____

ADDRESS: _____

CITY/TOWN: _____ PROVINCE: _____ CODE: _____

SIGNATURE:_____

Mail to: The Barbra Schlifer Commemorative Clinic Cookbook
        98 Chiltern Hill Road
        Toronto, Ontario
        M6C 3C1

— —

In Good Time

Please send me _____ copy/copies of IN GOOD TIME at $14.95 per copy plus
$2.00 for postage and handling. TOTAL $_____

    ☐ Cheque or money order payable to
       The Barbra Schlifer Commemorative Clinic

    ☐ Charge to Visa/Mastercard # _____
       Expiry Date   _____

NAME: _____

ADDRESS: _____

CITY/TOWN: _____ PROVINCE: _____ CODE: _____

SIGNATURE:_____

Mail to: The Barbra Schlifer Commemorative Clinic Cookbook
        98 Chiltern Hill Road
        Toronto, Ontario
        M6C 3C1